FASTING
THE MIND

"A highly intelligent and profound work sorely needed in our modern, over-stimulated world. Jason Gregory blends modern science and ancient spiritual wisdom to show us why mental overstimulation is so harmful. He then offers us a pathway to healing the mind, achieving emotional balance and moving deeper into true self-awareness. Enlightening and transformative on multiple levels. . . . a must-read for all seekers."

BRAD WILLIS (AKA BHAVA RAM),
FORMER NBC NEWS FOREIGN CORRESPONDENT
AND AUTHOR OF *WARRIOR POSE* AND *THE 8 LIMBS OF YOGA*

"I love 'mind fasting' because it gives us a fresh take on the word *meditation* and re-enlivens the concept of entering silence to rediscover our true, harmonious nature. Especially today, we need this reminder: Dive into boredom! Dump the need for speed! Delete distractions! Jason Gregory brings his wealth of historical and cross-cultural knowledge to this practice, making it interesting, simple, and doable."

PENNEY PEIRCE, AUTHOR OF *LEAP OF PERCEPTION* AND *FREQUENCY*

"Jason Gregory advises us to slow down, breathe, and embrace the silence at our core. Gregory is the White Rabbit of *Through the Looking Glass* who once advised Alice, 'Don't just do something, stand there.'"

DANA SAWYER, PROFESSOR OF RELIGION AND PHILOSOPHY
AT MAINE COLLEGE OF ART
AND AUTHOR OF *ALDOUS HUXLEY: A BIOGRAPHY*

"Who doesn't want a stronger more settled mind? No matter how enlightened you are or aren't this book will make you stop and think in new ways."

JASON NEMER, COFOUNDER OF ACROYOGA

"Fasting the mind is the missing link for embodying pure happiness and eliminating your stress and anxiety. This book is wise, deep, thorough, and well-researched. . . . Put down your smartphone and not only read this book, but *use* it! Get onto your personal path to inner peace, optimal health, and enlightenment—a return to your true nature—as you clear away all the interference."

LISA M. SELOW, AUTHOR OF *A REBEL CHICK MYSTIC'S GUIDE:*
HEALING YOUR SPIRIT WITH POSITIVE REBELLION

"*Fasting the Mind* discusses with depth and clarity one of the most important aspects of internal cultivation. . . . the mind must be disconnected from distracting stimuli in order for change to take place. Jason discusses with skill and accuracy why this is vital to our practice and places this ancient concept into a modern context. Vital reading. . . ."

DAMO MITCHELL, AUTHOR OF *WHITE MOON ON THE MOUNTAIN PEAK* AND *DAOIST NEI GONG*

"Stop distracting yourself, take time to breathe, and let this fascinating book soak in—your nervous system will thank you for it. *Fasting the Mind* is a treasure of a book in a world that so badly needs it."

KINGSLEY L. DENNIS, PH.D., AUTHOR OF *THE PHOENIX GENERATION: A NEW ERA OF CONNECTION, COMPASSION AND CONSCIOUSNESS*

"A mixture of modern-day science and astute scholarship gleaned from the ancient texts of wisdom cultures, *Fasting the Mind* contributes to the understanding of how the mind can be transformed from self-centeredness into an inseparable union with all that is . . . when consciousness lives with just what is. For the sake of all beings, we need to listen, ingest, and live this reality."

RODNEY SMITH, AUTHOR OF *AWAKENING: A PARADIGM SHIFT OF THE HEART*

"Goes straight to the point in language that is both thoughtful and uncompromising. . . . Slowing down, pulling back, checking indulgence, and paying attention allow us to smell the roses and appreciate the beauty and magic of life."

ROBERT SACHS, AUTHOR OF *BECOMING BUDDHA* AND *THE ECOLOGY OF ONENESS*

"*Fasting the Mind* in a word—incredible. It is the perfect book for calming the mind. . . . Jason offers wonderful techniques for achieving a free mind."

STEVEN L. HAIRFIELD, PH.D., AUTHOR OF *THE TWELVE SACRED PRINCIPLES OF KARMA*

"A concise, ambitious, and fascinating exploration of all things awakening. From social stress to our nervous system, the Vedas to Zen, Jason Gregory guides readers in a very accessible way to the truth of their being."

CHRIS GROSSO, AUTHOR OF *INDIE SPIRITUALIST* AND *EVERYTHING MIND*

FASTING
THE MIND

*Spiritual Exercises for
Psychic Detox*

JASON GREGORY

Inner Traditions
Rochester, Vermont • Toronto, Canada

Inner Traditions
One Park Street
Rochester, Vermont 05767
www.InnerTraditions.com

Library of Congress Cataloging-in-Publication Data

Names: Gregory, Jason, 1980– author.
Title: Fasting the mind : spiritual exercises for psychic detox / Jason Gregory.
Description: Rochester, Vermont : Inner Traditions, 2017. | Includes
  bibliographical references and index.
Identifiers: LCCN 2016048903 (print) | LCCN 2017007016 (e-book) |
  ISBN 9781620556467 (pbk.) | ISBN 9781620556474 (e-book)
Subjects: LCSH: Spiritual life. | Thought and thinking—Miscellanea. |
  Consciousness—Miscellanea.
Classification: LCC BL624 .G7335 2017 (print) | LCC BL624 (e-book) |
  DDC 204/.4—dc23
LC record available at https://lccn.loc.gov/2016048903

Printed and bound in the United States

10 9 8 7 6 5 4 3

Text design and layout by Priscilla Baker
This book was typeset in Garamond Premier Pro with Quicksand and Avant Garde used as display typefaces

To send correspondence to the author of this book, mail a first-class letter to the author c/o Inner Traditions • Bear & Company, One Park Street, Rochester, VT 05767, and we will forward the communication, or contact the author directly at **jasongregory.org**.

Dedicated to the ideal of a peaceful mind and a peaceful world. May this book be a step toward that ideal, which awaits all of us.

CONTENTS

ACKNOWLEDGMENTS

This book and its philosophy, methods, and practices are built on the shoulders of giants from both ancient and modern times. In the East especially, I am indebted to the great spiritual traditions and ancient masters who dedicated their lives to liberating the mind and humanity from suffering. Though we are thousands of years apart I'd like to humbly bow to those great masters of ancient times for having a direct impact on this book, especially Gautama the Buddha, Lao-tzu, Confucius, Mencius, Chuang-tzu, Patanjali, Bodhidharma, and Shankara. I would also like to bow in appreciation for those masters and teachers of modern times—both alive and dead—for influencing this book, especially Ramana Maharshi, Sri Yukteswar, Sri Aurobindo, Aldous Huxley, D. T. Suzuki, Alan Watts, Nisargadatta Maharaj, Sarvepalli Radhakrishnan, Joseph Campbell, Ananda Coomaraswamy, Jiddu Krishnamurti, Huston Smith, Shunryu Suzuki, Thomas Merton, Dalai Lama, S. N. Goenka, Thich Nhat Hanh, Ram Dass, Ken Wilber, Georg Feuerstein, William Hart, Richard E. Nisbett, Sadhguru Jaggi Vasudev, Mooji, and Edward Slingerland. Without the existence of any of these individuals this book never could have been realized.

Fasting the Mind could be published by no better publisher than Inner Traditions and Bear & Company. All of the wonderful people at this amazing publishing house understand the magnitude of this book and its importance in the modern world. I am beyond grateful to work with all of you. I am especially grateful to Jon Graham for his enthusiasm for this book and his great support of my work. Without you this book would never have reached its full potential or the hands of the readers. This brings me to Ehud Sperling, the brains behind Inner Traditions. Gratitude to you, Ehud, for understanding that there is still a place in the world for books that are deep and life changing. You have established a publishing house that stands alone in this world as a beacon of light guiding a peaceful future. Special gratitude must go to the two editors I worked with on *Fasting the Mind*. First to my copyeditor, Ben Gleason, I am astounded at your knack for picking up those minute errors in a book as only a gifted editor like yourself could do. You have made the text sparkle with clarity. Secondly, to my project editor, Meghan MacLean, you have been a blessing in the editing process of this book and my previous work. Your wisdom, not only in editing but also in understanding books such as mine, has allowed this book to reach a depth that it couldn't without you. I am extremely grateful to work with you.

This book was written in its entirety in Chiang Mai, Thailand. The Thai people were a constant motivation through the process of writing this book. I have learned a lot from the wonderful people of Thailand, and I am always blown away by the high level of respect and gratitude shown toward an outsider like myself. We could all learn a lot from that type of attitude.

To my lovely wife, Gayoung, special gratitude should be shared with you for being my closest teacher in this life. I have learned a lot from you and continue to do so every day. Not only are you engaged in the lifestyle that this book promotes, but you were also a source of inspiration that fuelled the words within this book. There is not a day that I am not grateful to be in your presence and experience the love we have for each other.

THE CURE IS ANCIENT

The epidemic of our times is not a war on terror or a war among nations and religions, nor is it any conflict between opposites that we can conceive of. It is a war so subtle that we are not even conscious of the battle being waged. It is a psychological war: a war against our mind, a war on consciousness. But this war is not being waged upon us from the outside world—at least not entirely so. The deep-down truth is that you have waged war upon yourself.

We are not even conscious of this fact because we are asleep at the wheel of our own life. We often play the victim card, as if the world is against us. In truth this mentality eclipses the real problem, which is that you are against yourself—not intentionally, but rather due to your inability to be your true and authentic self. This true and authentic self should not be confused with who you think you are as a personality. On the contrary, to be your true self means to reside in that deep place within your mind and heart where thoughts, feelings, and emotions are observed as temporary phenomena, like rising and crashing waves of the great ocean of consciousness.

Actually this is a more ancient view of ourselves, which comes out of the Indus Valley region of India, Pakistan, and Afghanistan.

From this region came the three great Hindu philosophical systems of Vedanta, Samkhya, and classical yoga. They gave birth to the two concepts known in Sanskrit as *Atman* and *Purusha*. *Atman* means the "Self"—with a capital *S*—in reference to the pure undifferentiated consciousness deep within us that is eternal, a pure state of awareness identical to the absolute ultimate reality of existence known in Sanskrit as *Brahman*. Likewise, Purusha refers to our original pure awareness that is untouched by anything the manifest universe produces and is essentially the eyes of Brahman.

We lose consciousness of our true self (Atman/Purusha) when we begin to believe we are the waves (personality) rather than the ocean (Brahman). The war we wage upon ourselves is from riding these waves of thoughts, feelings, and emotions, and ultimately the notion of separation. We believe these waves that we ride are permanent and lasting. Actually thoughts, feelings, and emotions are not really the problem because they are what color the world, making it beautiful or dramatic, bringing inspiration into the world when they are recognized in their truest context. That is, our thoughts, feelings, and emotions are temporary phenomena of sentient life, and they can be enjoyed if they are recognized as being temporary. So the real problem exists when we begin to identify with our thoughts, feelings, and emotions as if they are permanent and something that we can hold on to. We suffer as a result of this process. This suffering was one of the key aspects of human life that Gautama the Buddha realized. Buddha discovered that when we try to cling to our passing experiences, whether pleasurable or painful, we suffer. Armenian mystic George Ivanovich Gurdjieff had an interesting perspective and meditation on this matter of suffering:

> The sole means now for the saving of the beings of the planet Earth would be to implant again into their presences a new organ . . . of such properties that every one of these unfortunates during the process of existence should constantly sense and be cognizant of the inevitability of his own death as well as the death

everyone upon whom his eyes or attention rests. Only such a sensation and such a cognizance can now destroy the egoism completely crystallized in them.[1]

This is not to be thought of fatalistically. The real intention behind Gurdjieff's words is to liberate you from the impermanence of life and the illusion of this permanent ego, which you believe you are and which supposedly suffers from the impermanent roller coaster of life. Yet many people all over the world are addicted to riding this roller coaster, seeking pleasurable experiences without realizing that pain will inevitably come. People believe they are this "I," "me," "mine," and so on. As a result we become excessively self-interested. We try to sustain and maintain this permanent sense of "I," which in truth changes like the wind from moment to moment, with no permanent state. Trying to have the sense of a permanent self or ego in the face of the universal winds of change is a battle you will ultimately lose. No matter how hard you try to hold on to your idea of self, it can't be done.

If you remain the same person at sixty as you are at eighteen, that suggests that you may have some form of neurosis and psychosis. It is just not sane to believe you are this permanent person with all of these rigid beliefs about the world and yourself that drive the momentary pleasure you seek.

We may not recognize this, but the experiences we have that don't accord with our rigid beliefs can actually lead to a breakdown of our conditioning. We ignorantly call these experiences painful. Pain in this sense is actually a psychological shock to our ego that facilitates an evolution within our consciousness, a necessary dent in the armor of our ego that makes us realize—momentarily—that we are not in control of our life. We may be able to control the little incremental moments of our life, like where we left our car keys, but we cannot control what our personality wants, and it invariably gets what it needs, no matter whether we perceive that as a good thing or bad thing.

Sadly, many people believe they are in control of their lives, believing they are this permanent ego, containing all the dramas playing out within their thoughts, feelings, and emotions. As this tendency becomes stronger and stronger in our modern world, we see an exponential increase in mental health issues and psychological diseases. The medical industry doesn't seem to have any sort of cure for these problems other than medication like antidepressants, which only suppress the symptoms without addressing the root of the problem. As a result of how we orient ourselves toward the world, we believe the cure is something we acquire from the outside world. We need to reorient our attention to where the cure really is.

You possess the cure within yourself. But it is not some form of magic, hypnosis, or trickery. It is actually a natural way of life that we must come back into resonance with. This is much easier said than done, because it requires discipline to resist what stimulates us. None of these problems are new; we've had them since the dawn of human civilization. And they were more recognizable in ancient times because the world was not as complex as it is today. This simplicity in ancient times is what allowed a cure for our mind and all of its acquired issues to arise. The ancient ultimate cure was born in the East, and it is a method of discipline and practice that we fear in our modern world.

THE ANCIENT METHOD OF MIND FASTING

The method and practice born in the East is known as mind fasting or fasting the mind. Mind fasting directly impacts the habits and tendencies of our subconscious, which in turn affects our lifestyle. This method was born mainly in the Indus Valley region on the borders of modern-day India, Pakistan, Afghanistan, and also in the Yellow River valley of China, going back to at least 2000 BCE. I will discuss the origins of mind fasting later in this book.

The peoples of both ancient China and ancient India suffered just as we do from the excessive demands of daily life. It may appear that their individual and social problems were small in comparison to ours psychologically, but back in those times there was always the daily struggles to survive against the real threat of environmental conditions. Mind fasting put people's anxieties at ease back in those ancient times so they could see with clarity the way forward, not only individually, but also collectively. This is why this ancient method of healing is imperative for us to rediscover in our modern era.

In the ancient East people sensitive to their lives realized that their social and cultural problems stem from the lifestyle choices they made on an individual level. In those times, just as today, many people suffered because they were self-interested, and their selfish lifestyle reflected their egocentric attitude. People began to believe it was them versus the world, without realizing they are part of something much bigger than themselves, whether as part of society, culture, humanity, a religion, God, or the universe. It doesn't matter because the idea is that we recognize that we are part of something much greater than ourselves. When our awareness is directed in this way, we begin to act without self-interest and ultimately harmonize with the greater totality. Acting in this way not only makes a healthy society, but also sane individuals. This doesn't mean giving up following our interests; on the contrary, what it does mean is that we are not attached to our interests or their outcomes. Instead, we do things because we sincerely love them, and love seeks nothing but itself.

In the Indian spiritual epic, the *Bhagavad Gita,* the godly sage Krishna is trying to teach the worldly warrior Arjuna this unattached attitude that is supposed to lead to bliss, *ananda* in Sanskrit. In the *Bhagavad Gita* Krishna tries to persuade Arjuna to go into battle against his beloved family, friends, and revered teachers to fulfill his duty without being lost in the superficial, emotional details of who they are. In this sense Krishna tries to compel Arjuna to yield to the divine will and follow his *dharma* (meaning "virtue" or "God-given duty") as a warrior. Essentially, Krishna wants Arjuna to play his role in the Divine's cosmic theater, which we call life. In this passage there is an emphasis on the Sanskrit term *nishkam karma*, which means "not being attached to the fruit of your action." The *Bhagavad Gita* states:

> To action alone hast thou a right and never at all to its fruits; let not the fruits of action be thy motive; neither let there be in thee any attachment to inaction.
>
> Fixed in yoga, do thy work, O Winner of wealth (Arjuna), abandoning attachment, with an even mind in success and failure, for evenness of mind is called yoga.[2]

In not being attached to our volition we are not self-interested. We also lose the attachment to striving for goals. In both cases our egocentric self-interest ultimately makes us suffer because it constantly fuels this striving to attain goals, which in many cases are unattainable. Inadvertently, as a result, our volition becomes part of an unfolding process of life, which is linked to that which is greater than you as a person. This means that every individual's latent dharma (virtue) is unique and has the potential to inspire the world, but paradoxically not when we are egocentric. When we have the idea of a person separate from the whole then this leads to all sorts of conflict, not only between individuals but also tribal conflicts, which in the modern era are wars between different cultures, nations, and religions.

The great sages of the East were aware of this tendency for people to slip into the wrong perception of seeing themselves as separate from the world and universe around them. This wrong perception leads to habits of mind and lifestyle that are self-interested and driven by seeking pleasure. The sages recognized that such a lifestyle is centered on pursuing excessive stimulation, as if momentary pleasure is lasting. We all know what happens to our physical body when we seek excessive stimulation. Our body becomes unhealthy, we become fat, and we harm our internal organs, which reduces our life span as a result. In ancient times, and somewhat still in the modern era, when a physician would examine a sick individual and realize that their lifestyle choices were leading to bad eating habits centered around momentary pleasures, they would offer the radical prescription of physically fasting the body so that all of the internal organs could finally be given the time to rest and repair from the damage done by such excess.

The poor old body has become the victim of a mind that is constantly agitated. Fasting the body helps it repair itself, and we begin to correct our bad eating habits. As a result we cultivate new, healthy habits that contribute to well-being and longevity. And so we change a part of our lifestyle, but only a part. The great sages of the East realized that. They understood that fasting the body is great and can have a wonderful effect on our mind and life. But bodily fasting in no way ceases the mind's excessive need to do, to achieve, to strive, and to be a person who is self-interested, all of which lead to the psychological bad habits that drive our suffering, including our diets. The great sages of the East, then, were not concerned with fasting the body; instead they were concerned with fasting the mind.

WHAT IS MIND FASTING?

Mind fasting has a direct impact on the root cause of all our suffering. Fasting the mind is the process of eliminating all the content that stimulates our mind and refraining from the habit of trying to stimulate it out of fear of boredom. Yet boredom exists only because we have become so accustomed to distracting our mind with stimulation. A sage would say we need to dive into our boredom without falling back into the habit of seeking stimulation, because according to them boredom has a secret to teach us. Boredom is a cognitive response we begin to have when we starve the mind of its usual diet of habitual thoughts. The sage's secret is that if we can starve the mind—fast the mind—then we will begin to feel a state of equanimity that is not dependent on excessive stimulation. By dealing with our boredom through fasting the mind we begin to feel that sense of unity within, the Atman and Purusha, which the agitation of boredom eclipses. Fasting the mind means we don't respond to any sensations like boredom.

Fasting the mind is the ultimate cure to suffering because, as with fasting the body, we have given the mind time to truly relax from any sort of stimulation so it can repair itself and come back into equilibrium. In fasting the mind we come back to our original true nature, not as individual persons, but instead as the entire universe as it exists deep within—Atman and Purusha that is eclipsed by mental activity. From this deep nature within we begin to act authentically and carry out the spontaneous functions of the universe that exist in our unconscious and manifest as our dharma. This is what will lead to real world peace, because the individual has come into resonance with the actuality of the universe. Individual, social, and cultural harmony comes into being as a result, and a real spirituality is recognized.

The only thing that stops this from becoming our reality is you. If you don't take fasting the mind seriously you will continue to distract your mind with whatever frivolous nonsense is available while you continue to complain about your suffering and the suffering of the world. We truly cannot complain if we do not take responsibility for what our mind consumes. Likewise with our diet, if we do not take responsibility for what we eat then we cannot complain about being fat. Only you can help yourself, which inadvertently changes the world. In the same fashion, this book will give you the knowledge, wisdom, and tools to truly heal through the ancient art and science of fasting the mind. A thorough examination of your habitual patterns and lifestyle is required on your behalf. The time to refrain from all distractions and begin the great fast is now.

1

THE NEED FOR
SPEED IS SUICIDE

Just stop everything you are doing right now! Stop thinking, stop planning, stop competing, stop comparing, and just breathe deeply for a minute. Now breathe for another minute. There—I have your undivided attention. For much of our life our attention is divided because we lack the awareness to just stop our mind from its incessant activity and movement. We act compulsively from the activity of our mind without being able to observe it from a distance. As a result, we constantly respond only to our unconscious mental agitation. We feel that if we are not doing something then we have no purpose, and so we become anxious and stressful. We are trying to achieve one thing after another after another after another with no end in sight.

We become addicted to doing without truly knowing how to relax our mind deeply. Our mind has become accustomed to being anxious, stressful, and agitated because we don't know how to stop the madness. Oh, and we need to be clear here: it surely is madness to be incessantly thinking and acting on those thoughts. Our world reflects this madness.

SOCIAL STRESS IS INDIVIDUAL ANXIETY
AND VICE VERSA

It is increasingly difficult for people to deal with the demands of society. The social structure that is built around us in this world demands that the individual continually strive to achieve innumerable goals in the vain hope of one day achieving success. Yet the success that some of us taste is like fairy gold: once we attain it, whatever we think is success turns out to be worthless—a gold that we cannot touch, taste, or feel, and in the end is only momentary, leaving us with a feeling of deflated emptiness. As a result, we try even harder to climb more mountains under the belief that at the top there will be real gold. But we only continue to find fairy gold. This is an absurd approach to life that we have all subscribed to. Real success is not about achieving goals as if they are ends themselves. Success is really about being at ease in your everyday life, where the process is more important than the goal.

Being at peace in your life is what success is about, but to realize that you need to completely appreciate the process of it. We need to think of our life in terms of a dance. What's more important: getting to the end of the dance, or the process of the dance itself? We all know the answer but we don't apply this wise insight to our daily life. Instead we strive toward what society believes success to be, which ultimately ties us in knots. We then think that to untie these knots we need to put our foot on the accelerator in our life. This is a recipe for disaster. There is no way to bring peace to your life by making yourself busier. A real feeling of success will never be achieved that way. Real success will be recognized only when we alleviate all of our stress and anxiety so we can approach life with a peaceful mind that is not perturbed by what we believe our daily struggles are.

But we are not taught to be that way. Our world unintentionally—or perhaps even intentionally—prevents our finding peace, because to do so requires us to refrain from exerting so much effort to achieve anything personally. We have to cease striving, no matter how noble or compelling we believe the so-called goal to be. Once we stop trying so hard, we will discover the power and success we truly want, even though we didn't know it existed. We find this wisdom going far back to ancient times in the East. This counterintuitive approach to life is not accepted nor promoted in our modern world.

From birth, our parents, friends, and schools teach us that if we want to be successful we need to do a lot of hard work. We essentially need to make ourselves busy, busy, busy. As a result from living our life this way we feel similar to the feeling we get from listening to the track "You Spin Me Round (Like a Record)" by British pop band Dead or Alive—like we're so dizzy, we don't know which direction is up.

We are spinning psychologically out of control because we multitask in every minute of our life. The mental load we carry becomes a weight so great that we can shrug it off only when we stop the madness. We need to discover a way to slow down in the midst of this chaos within our mind. If we don't take our foot off the gas we are going to drive off the cliff's edge into social and individual insanity. This is no idle threat or poetic way to describe our current plight as a species. It is a real danger that is already taking place.

THE GLOBAL PANIC ATTACK

The war we wage against ourselves is caused by overfilling our cup. We pack everything into our life, leaving no time for our mind to truly rest. We bombard our mind from every direction. The excessive busyness from multitasking all day—with digital devices everywhere, incessantly and mindlessly chatting all day—keeps us in a state of hypnosis that replicates sleep. Our conscious mind has no time even to notice our breathing. The constant bombardment of mental stimuli has numbed our senses and put us to sleep. This sleeplike state resembles the psychosis of serial killers and demagogues, yet it actually afflicts most of us. In books and films this state is represented metaphorically by zombies and the undead.

Some of the zombies in our world are our leaders, politicians. We expect critical judgments and efficient decisions from people who have their eyes open but are actually asleep. Think about it: some of the busiest people in the world are politicians, potentially the most unaware and asleep people in the world. And yet we rely on them to make big decisions for the welfare of humanity. This explains why many politicians are still hypnotically self-interested, without any real concern for the greater community: in reality the lights are on but nobody is home. I have nothing against the role of the politician; it is just one example to accentuate what happens when we fill our cup with busyness.

In the ancient Chinese philosophy of Taoism, which originated from the great sage Lao-tzu and his classic text the *Tao Te Ching,* there is a focus on emptying your cup. In the *Tao Te Ching* Lao-tzu explains that when our cup is full we lose awareness of the Tao. *Tao* is a Chinese word referring to the Way or path of the irreducible essence of the universe that we feel in our experience, making us feel completely alive and present in the eternal now. He believes our struggles and suffering come from the "mind-cup" being too full of distractions and the busyness of thinking. Lao-tzu emphasizes that we should begin the process of emptying our mind-cup. He believes real wisdom is born in an empty mind. In fact, he would take it one step further by saying the empty mind is our real nature and this is how a sane person functions. In Taoist philosophy there are a few analogies to articulate Lao-tzu's point. For example, when we look at a cup, what is more valuable: the cup or the space within the cup? Likewise with a house, what is more valuable, the walls of the house or the space within the house? The answer for both is surely the space, because without space to experience life there is no point in having either a cup or house. You couldn't experience life without space, and this is Lao-tzu's wisdom.

Gautama the Buddha also discovered the importance of this mental space, as it is impossible to be truly awake without it. He stripped the content and beliefs from his mind to see reality as it truly is. This enlightened state of the Buddha is something rare in our modern world because enlightenment is incorrectly thought of as constructing a life worth living, rather than deconstructing your life to make the process of living an end in itself. In filling our empty cup we try to construct a life that is always geared toward the future without ever being present in the now. The result of such perception is suffering, as we are never content with the way life is. We ignore the wisdom of the wise and continue to follow social convention even though we know it doesn't lead to everlasting happiness. By filling our mind-cup more and more we are slowly but surely destroying ourselves.

These destructive tendencies are even more evident in our modern era than in ancient times. With excessive information, content, and stimuli, mental health issues are on the increase, and we have no idea why. One reason for this is because we rarely take into account our lifestyle, which is the primary focus of ancient Eastern medical systems such as ayurveda in India and traditional Chinese medicine (TCM) in China. If our life is out of balance, then from the point of view of Eastern medicine we need to change the habitual patterns of our mind and begin to slow down. From the perspective of TCM our inability to slow down results from an overexertion of *yang* (masculine, active, doing, hot energy) at the expense of *yin* (feminine, receptive, nondoing, cool energy). This results in a culture that is yin deficient and heading for both internal and external calamities. Essentially this is an overheated system from excessive motion within the mind and body. If we don't slow down then mental health issues are inevitable.

Our modern understanding and approach to healing our psychological crises is all wrong. Prescription drugs only suppress the symptom without addressing the root cause. Our stress and anxiety are truly lifestyle diseases born in an unsettled mind. Many people suffer from these diseases, but we never seem to cure them of their psychological ailments. Stress and anxiety go on untreated. As a result our mind-cups begin to crack, which manifests as panic attacks, anxiety attacks, schizophrenia, and so on.

Just think about how common panic attacks are these days. Lots of people have experienced at least one in their life, often without any awareness of why it occurred. Panic attacks happen because we don't slow down our mental activity. A panic attack essentially is your nervous system hitting the brakes, since you won't consciously stop yourself. We take on employment that keeps us super busy all day long, and then we go home to all our digital devices that overstimulate our senses while we are under the illusion that we are relaxing or being entertained. Add to that the constant idle chitchat and gossip people churn out daily. Panic attacks are inevitable when we are anxious all the time. The mind really has no time to rest and be silent. As the Zen Buddhist master Thich Nhat Hanh explains, we are essentially like cows ruminating on food continually. The food that we ruminate on is our mental activity, and it leads to all sorts of psychological problems. Thich Nhat Hanh states in his book *Silence*:

> All the sounds around us and all the thoughts that we're constantly replaying in our minds can be thought of as a kind of food. We're familiar with edible food, the kind of food we physically chew and swallow. But that's not the only kind of food we humans consume; it's just one kind. What we read, our conversations, the shows we watch, the online games we play, and our worries, thoughts, and anxieties are all food. No wonder we often don't have space in our consciousness for beauty and silence: we are constantly filling up on so many other kinds of food.
>
> Even if we are not talking with others, reading, listening to the radio, watching television, or interacting online, most of us don't feel settled or quiet.[1]

We're constantly under mental attack and we don't even know it. We believe that in constantly entertaining ourselves we are happy. Nothing could be farther from the truth. Many people are enslaved by what they view as entertainment. For example, many people cannot go one day without checking their phone or e-mail or social media networks. If we cannot go one day without these then are we free or are we more enslaved than ever? When mobile devices, smartphones, the Internet, and social media were created we thought they would make us happier because we would be more connected. But it has had the reverse effect. Being so connected has made us more anxious and stressful.

We no longer want to go for a quiet walk or sit peacefully in the park without our phones. We are distraction junkies. We are not really that fascinated by our phone or its content: we are just addicted to distracting our mind from experiencing reality as it is. There is definitely no need for any of us to be checking our phones, e-mail, and social media every day. None of us are that popular. There are many examples of famous and successful people who don't need those things to create remarkable art. For example, the English-American Hollywood director and writer Christopher Nolan has achieved great success without a mobile phone or e-mail account. Because he is not distracted by these things, he can create the great films he is known for. If we followed his example and allowed space to come into our life, rather than filling it up full of distractions, then imagine the spontaneous creativity that would explode from our mind.[2]

We can achieve this latent potential within us through fasting the mind. Real, everlasting freedom is our original nature, but we can recognize it only when the mind has completely fasted. The freedom we thought we would achieve through being more connected with our digital devices is just more fairy gold. Being more connected has the opposite effect to what we expected, making us more anxious with the ever-impending doom of waiting for the next Facebook message or tweet. Being so anxious invariably leads to panic attacks. All of this panic, both individually and globally, is caused by our leading psychologically unhealthy lifestyles that affect us to the core of our being. We are headed for a head-on collision with the natural rhythm of the universe because we can't take our foot off the accelerator.

The continuation or annihilation of our species depends on the psychological state of the individual, and that state is currently undergoing cardiac arrest. We believe that these distractions and the constant rumi-nating on our mental activity is a way for humanity to evolve. Yet what society offers instead does far more damage than we think. Mental dis-ease will continue to increase if we don't become more conscious about what our mind is consuming. We might think we can fix the damage by changing just a few small habits, but it's much more complicated than that. We are actually encountering the decay of our nervous system through the process of incessantly consuming external stimuli, which keeps our mind numbed and neurotic. The cure for our nervous sys-tem is a fasting of the mind so intense that our complete psychosomatic organism can heal itself back to its original nature.

2

WAR ON THE
NERVOUS SYSTEM

The war we wage upon ourselves through external and internal stimuli depletes our nervous system. When we deplete our nervous system our mind becomes susceptible to mental illness. The busier we are without resting our nervous system the more chances we have of developing psychological diseases. If we are going to fill our mind-cups so much that they overflow, then we have to drastically change our mentality and lifestyle from the ground up. A physician cannot cure this with prescription drugs that only sedate you.

The responsibility is on you to have the strength to change your habitual patterns and slow down the pace of your life. If we don't then we run the very real risk of living in a world where people are primarily not conscious in their everyday lives, which will ultimately lead to unconscious acts of violence based on individual self-interest and group-think mentality. Acting unconsciously, we are like a pack of wolves operating from the animalistic mode of protection and security, which is driven by fear. One must wonder if we are not already halfway to that point. Nevertheless, as human beings we have a choice to change right now, which will guide us in the right direction of health toward a love that is real and not based on associations with people and groups. Jesus experienced this real love, revealed by his instruction to love your neighbor as much as you love your family. To come to that place of wisdom we need a drastic method for slowing down our nervous system and its habitual need to do something, a habit that we have become accustomed to from repeated anxiousness in the mind.

The addiction to being in motion and incessantly doing things is not a new temperament. This problem existed in the East in ancient times, though maybe not as intense as today. Yet the ancient Asian cultures thought of things differently than we do today: they understood that mental and physical health and well-being is built on a lifestyle that is peaceful and virtuous. There was a direct focus on completely relaxing the nervous system, which allows us to come into resonance with something much greater than ourselves, leading to wisdom and the psychological state of enlightenment.

THE ANCIENT EASTERN SCIENCE
OF THE NERVOUS SYSTEM

The spiritual path of Buddhism came into existence as a result of this yearning to completely slow down our nervous system so we can experience real freedom. In Sanskrit such freedom is called *nirvana,* meaning extinction, freedom from suffering, and ultimately the unconditioned eternal reality that we experience as enlightenment. In the story of Gautama the Buddha, he sought methods of practice and philosophy that would evoke the state of nirvana. He followed asceticism and strict spiritual practices for six years. It wasn't until he was exhausted in his efforts that he finally took some milky soup from a young girl herding cattle and sat under the famous Bodhi tree in the small town of Bodh Gaya, India. In doing so, he completely relaxed without the need for striving. His original efforts had been futile because he was approaching enlightenment in the same way that we purchase a cheap suit. In striving for anything, there is still agitation in the mind, and this perception of life comes from the ignorant view of how we supposedly achieve things in this world.

Whether knowingly or unknowingly, Gautama the Buddha accessed a part of our nervous system that remains dormant when we are always in physical and mental motion. This part of our nervous system is known as the parasympathetic nervous system (PSNS).

To gain a better understanding of this we need to know what makes up the nervous system. The nervous system is the part of an animal's body that coordinates its voluntary and involuntary actions and also transmits signals to and from different parts of its body. In vertebrate species, such as human beings, the nervous system contains two parts, the central nervous system (CNS) and the peripheral nervous system (PNS). The central nervous system contains the brain and spinal cord, while the peripheral nervous system consists of mainly nerves, which are enclosed bundles of long fibers, and axons, which are long, slender projections of nerve cells that conduct electrical impulses away from the neuron's cell body. These nerves and axons connect the central nervous system to every other part of the body. The peripheral nervous system is divided into the somatic nervous system (SoNS) and the autonomic nervous system (ANS).

The autonomic nervous system is our central focus when related to psychological or spiritual inner work and transformation. The autonomic nervous system is a control system that largely acts unconsciously and regulates our bodily functions such as heart rate, respiratory rate, digestion, pupillary response, urination, and sexual arousal. The autonomic nervous system has two branches: the sympathetic nervous system (SNS) and the parasympathetic nervous system (PSNS). The sympathetic nervous system is sometimes considered the "fight or flight" system because it is activated in cases of emergencies to mobilize energy. It is what we activate when we are in motion and being stimulated through our senses. Without it we could not do anything. The parasympathetic nervous system, on the other hand, is often considered the "rest and digest" or "feed and breed" system because it is activated when we are in a relaxed state. We activate the parasympathetic nervous system when we essentially do nothing. It is also responsible for stimulation of "rest and digest" and "feed and breed" activities that occur when the body is at rest, especially after eating, including sexual arousal, lacrimation (tears), salivation, urination, digestion, and defecation. The parasympathetic nervous system is what makes us drift off to sleep every night. It is stimulated most when we relax deeply.

The war on our nervous system is essentially the overstimulation of our sympathetic nervous system along with an understimulation of the parasympathetic nervous system. When we stimulate only the sympathetic nervous system without activating the parasympathetic nervous system, we increase the probability of chemical imbalances in our brain from not having a healthy balanced lifestyle. Because of this, the vast majority of us are teetering on the edge of psychological suicide.

People may say in response to this statement that they have time to relax every day. But are our methods for relaxation really relaxing? Our perception of relaxing is sitting in front of the television or computer, playing with our phones, chatting with friends, and so on. This is not true relaxation. Actually, when we engage in such activities we are still stimulating the sympathetic nervous system and not the parasympathetic nervous system. Accessing the parasympathetic nervous system requires a complete shutdown and withdrawal of the senses and mental activity, known as *pratyahara* in Sanskrit. This shutdown is important to Hinduism, Taoism, and especially Buddhism with its methods of practicing meditation.

No matter whether it is Theravada, Mahayana, Vajrayana, or Zen, the various strands of the Buddha's teachings have at their core the necessity of starving or fasting the mind. This is done to allow the parasympathetic nervous system to play its role within our psychosomatic organism. One of the more effective methods that the Buddha supposedly taught was *vipassana*. *Vipassana* is a Pali word (*vipasyana* in Sanskrit) used in the Buddhist tradition that means "insight into the true nature of reality." The meditation practice of vipassana is an ancient method that is believed to have come from Gautama the Buddha himself and which survived through other Buddhas throughout history. Vipassana meditation is thought of not only as a meditation practice in all life but also a disciplined technique that is supposed to evoke vipassana in all life. This technique was reintroduced by Burmese Theravada Buddhist teachers Ledi Sayadaw and Mogok Sayadaw. It was then popularized by Mahasi Sayadaw (a Burmese Theravada Buddhist monk and meditation master), Saya Gi U Ba Khin (the Burmese vipassana meditation teacher and an influential leader of the vipassana movement), and his student, Satya Narayan Goenka (better known as S. N. Goenka), who is well known for spreading the vipassana movement worldwide with more than a hundred centers located in various countries around the world.

The vipassana meditation technique is like shock therapy for your nervous system, consisting of a ten-day course in seclusion away from worldly distractions, where you meditate for hours each day, eat small portions of vegetarian food, and sleep, with no talking at all for the whole duration. The effect this has on us is immense. During the ten days people are finally giving themselves the chance to allow the parasympathetic nervous system to function without the interference of the sympathetic nervous system habitually seeking stimulation. The result is that a lot of the subconscious content lying dormant within our nervous system—content that drives our unconscious reactions and responses to the world—rises to the surface of our conscious mind, giving us the opportunity to finally reveal and heal our deep-seated conditioning.

Vipassana meditation practitioner William Hart explains how we can use "right awareness" and the awareness of respiration (*anapanasati* in Pali and *anapanasmrti* in Sanskrit) to bring us back into the ultimate reality of the here and now. He shows how, through the awareness of respiration we can start observing the normally unconscious autonomic functioning of the psychosomatic organism. In Hart's book *The Art of Living: Vipassana Meditation* he states:

Focusing on breathing can help us explore whatever is unknown about ourselves, to bring into consciousness whatever has been unconscious. It acts as a bridge between the conscious and unconscious mind, because the breath functions both consciously and unconsciously. We can decide to breathe in a particular way, to control the respiration. We can even stop breathing for a time. And yet when we cease trying to control respiration, it continues without any prompting.

For example, we may begin by breathing intentionally, slightly hard, in order to fix the attention more easily. As soon as the awareness of respiration becomes clear and steady, we allow the breath to proceed naturally, either hard or soft, deep or shallow, long or short, fast or slow. We make no effort to regulate the breath; the effort is only to be aware of it.[1]

Observing our conscious, intentional breath leads us to awareness of the normally unconscious, autonomic function of our natural breath. This meditation on the breath guides us beyond superficial reality toward an awareness of a subtle reality, while the illusion of past and future eclipses this awareness of a subtle reality. Human suffering stems from the looming anxiety of the future and the stress from our past experiences. This temperament has us obsessing about ourselves in an unconscious "me, me, me"–centered attitude. As a result our mind is often lost in the fantasies and illusions of the past and future, where we hold on to pleasant experiences while trying to erase unpleasant experiences of the past, without realizing that both will stay dormant within the subconscious if they are not brought to the surface of consciousness.

When we are mindlessly out of sync with the here and now we are unaware of the cravings and aversions that our subconscious continues to fuel and that drive our unconscious reactions toward the world. Anapanasati is an advanced method that will deliver us from this dilemma of suffering and the perpetual subconscious obsession we have about ourselves. The awareness of respiration, especially if practiced earnestly throughout our life, will allow us to be ever present in the here and now effortlessly, without the need for trying. But this might not be the case in the beginning because we have become accustomed to distraction over the course of our lives. Some effort, then, is necessary at the start of disciplining our attention to be focused in the present moment.

Vipassana is a flawless method for digging into the unconscious material within our mind to give us a glimpse of our true nature. The only problem with this method of fasting the mind is what to do with it when we come out of seclusion and return to the world. American mythologist Joseph Campbell called this "bringing back the boon," referring to anybody who chooses to break away from fear to embark on the "hero's journey" and then return to the world to share what they have learned. Campbell explains:

> The whole idea is that you've got to bring out again that which you went to recover, the unrealized, unutilized potential in yourself. The whole point of this journey is the reintroduction of this potential into the world; that is to say, to you living in the world. You are to bring this treasure of understanding back and integrate it in a rational life. It goes without saying, this is very difficult. Bringing the boon back can be even more difficult than going down into your own depths in the first place.[2]

Many people who come out of a vipassana course often fall straight back into familiar habits when they return to their usual surroundings. The constant practice of fasting the mind hasn't taken root yet because people fall back into the habit of excessive stimulation. When we get back into that habit we begin to overuse the sympathetic nervous system again. Few people, no matter whether they have done a vipassana meditation course, are conscious of how they consume and transform energy taken in through the nervous system.

HUMAN ENERGY CONSUMPTION

The methods of fasting the mind, such as vipassana, are supposed to make us more aware of the sensations in our body and how they are linked to the mind. The practice of vipassana facilitates a special kind of vision related to sensations. This special vision involves the cultivation of the ability to observe the reality within ourselves by focusing our attention objectively on the sensations within the body. The more we focus on our sensations the more we begin to become conscious of their psychosomatic origins. When we have sustained attention on our bodily sensations we are essentially infiltrating the storehouse of the subconscious and its unconscious content. The reason for this is because everything we experience in life, either mental or physical, leaves an imprint within the depths of our consciousness that has the potential to drive future sensations unconsciously.

Sensations are produced when we come into contact with the outside physical world. Likewise with the mind, when we have the mental experience of thoughts, emotions, feelings, ideas, imaginations, hopes, and fears, sensations are produced with no physical object driving them. But they are somewhat based on the mental images of a past experience we had in the external world. These mental images of the past fuel our imagination, which drives our aspirations for the future. Sensations, then, are not isolated to what we experience in the external world. They are the resonance between the body and mind flowing through our nervous system. In general, people tend to react to sensations both consciously and unconsciously without ever observing them objectively or questioning their origins.

The practice of anapanasati allows us to be cognizant of the intrinsic connection of the body and mind through the awareness of sensations that bind them together, which gives us the ability and vision to observe and dive deep into our unconscious content. This allows us to really heal on a fundamental level because we have uncovered those aspects of our psyche that were repressed and suppressed.

William Hart alludes to this in his research of vipassana meditation practice:

> Sensations occur at all times throughout the body. Every contact, mental or physical, produces a sensation. Every biochemical reaction gives rise to sensation. In ordinary life, the conscious mind lacks the focus necessary to be aware of all but the most intense of them, but once we have sharpened the mind by the practice of *anapana-sati* and thus developed the faculty of awareness, we become capable of experiencing consciously the reality of every sensation within.[3]

During a vipassana course we definitely do become more consciously aware of the sensations rising and falling within our psychosomatic organism. Yet as I've mentioned, when people go back into their familiar environments they easily fall back into the deep-seated habits of their past. The reason for this is ten days is not enough to dismantle a lifetime of conditioning.

Our nervous system has become so accustomed to our habits and the energy that we consume that it requires a monumental effort to begin to transmute such latent conditioning. In becoming more sensitive to our psychosomatic organism we should be more conscious of how we consume energy, which we transform into our life experiences. But we often remain unconscious because we are in the trap of using only our sympathetic nervous system, so we are perpetually attracted to actively being in motion and doing things either physically or mentally. Invariably we seek out what nourishes this habitual temperament. In order to be more conscious and to break these habits we need to understand how we consume and transform energy on the human level.

We consume energy in three primary ways: the food and liquid we ingest, the air we breathe, and the impressions we take in through the eyes and ears. What we take in through these three ways of consuming energy is what we transform into our conscious experience. We consume sensory energy through our five senses, which in turn stimulates

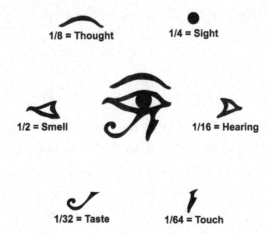

1/8 = Thought

1/4 = Sight

1/2 = Smell

1/16 = Hearing

1/32 = Taste

1/64 = Touch

Figure 2.1. The eye of Horus six-sense philosophy. By Dao Stew.

our sixth sense, thoughts. This energy reaches our senses through the physical orifices, or "nine gates" of the human instrument, which are the two eyes, two ears, two nostrils, mouth, anus, and penis or vagina. The concepts of the six senses and nine gates are actually older esoteric knowledge from India and Egypt, and they are illustrated in the Eye of Horus, known in Egyptian as the Wadjet (see figure 2.1).

In my book *Enlightenment Now* I explained that if we do not guard the nine gates with pure awareness, then our six senses are susceptible to attack. It becomes a priority to be more conscious of the energy we consume, as this will affect our nervous system in either a positive or negative way. It is hard, however, for many people in the modern world to consume clean sensory energy and guard their nine gates unless they are conscious of this knowledge. Many of us live a life that is extremely busy and our sympathetic nervous system is always depleted. The energy we consume reflects our mentality.

For example, many of us live in cities and breathe toxic air. Many people are so busy with their day job that they believe they have no time to make healthy food at home, and as a result they eat fast food and quench their thirst with sugary soft drinks, which are like sugar bombs. And as a result of breathing bad air and eating and drinking bad food all day, people come home to fill their eyes and ears full of noise from the numerous digital devices available. We are hypnotically attracted to nonsense on television and mindlessly scrolling through social media feeds. This activity is more akin to the devious temperament of acquisitiveness than anything else. It is not really hard for people to break these habits when we become dedicated and more conscious from practicing the fasting the mind discipline. If we think it is too hard to embrace a new way, that is really just a cop-out.

There is always a way, but we have to begin to activate the parasympathetic nervous system and consume cleaner mental energy. It requires us to examine our life and lifestyle choices by becoming more disciplined so our mind doesn't drift off into old habits. If we don't choose to alleviate old habits we will continue to have disease arise in our mind and body.

Because we have been raised in an ignorant world that promotes the activation of only the sympathetic nervous system, we seek distraction to numb our mind by perpetually being active. Yet what we are choosing to sedate us is still stimulating the sympathetic nervous system on a subtle level. No matter what we choose to chill out with, whether it is television, social media feeds, or idle chitchat, in reality we are still agitating our mind covertly. And because we are distracted easily in a sleeplike state, we invariably choose to consume toxic energy because we are completely unconscious.

Thich Nhat Hanh explains a thorough approach to living happy and healthy in the face of the constant bombardment of toxic energy with the teaching of the *four nutriments* of Buddhism, which is extremely similar in scope to the six-sense philosophy and the nine gates of ancient India and Egypt. The four nutriments are based on the Buddhist knowledge that every person consumes four kinds of "food" every day: literal, edible food; sense impressions received through our eyes, ears, and so on; volition, that is, your will, your desires, without which you would simply never do anything; and consciousness, meaning both individual and collective consciousness. But these foods can have all sorts of effects on our mind, as Thich Nhat Hanh explains:

All of these foods can be healthy or unhealthy, nourishing or toxic, depending on what we consume, how much we consume, and how aware we are of our consumption. For example, we sometimes eat junk food that makes us sick, or drink too much when we're upset about something, in the hopes of distracting ourselves even if afterward that consumption makes us feel worse.

We do the same thing with the other nutriments. With sensory food, we may have the awareness to take in media that are wholesome and enlightening, or on the other hand we may use video games, movies, magazines, or even engaging in gossip in order to distract ourselves from our suffering. Volition can also be healthy (constructive motivation) or unhealthy (craving and obsession). Likewise, collective consciousness can be healthy or unhealthy. Think of how affected you are by the mood or the consciousness of the group you are in, whether that group is supportive, happy, angry, gossipy, competitive, or listless.

Because each nutriment affects us so deeply, it's important to be aware of what and how much we are consuming. Our awareness is the key to our protection. Without protection, we absorb far too many toxins. Without realizing it, we become full of toxic sounds and toxic consciousness that makes us ill.[4]

Consuming toxic energy leads to more distractions, as Thich Nhat Hanh explained, causing the task of fasting the mind to appear insurmountable. We continue to apply more toxic layers over our mind to the point where we have lost connection with who we truly are within, beneath our identity. For those few who have begun to shed these layers through extensive spiritual self-work, it can be hard to deal with the majority of people who remain distracted. This is not because they are bad people, but instead because of the tension you feel in them. This tension you feel in them through their conversations and the way they carry themselves through life. They are not at ease as a result of stimulating only the sympathetic nervous system. The tension created from this overstimulation imprisons them within the boundaries of their habitual thoughts. To alleviate this tension we have to be sincere in refraining from distractions because they numb the senses and stupefy the mind.

ADDICTED TO THE DOPE

British philosopher Alan Watts once said, "We are addicted to the dope." He didn't mean we were addicted to marijuana or any other psychoactive substance. What he meant was we have become addicted to what stupefies the mind, essentially what makes us dopey. Distraction junkies are addicted to the dope. We are essentially addicted to the feeling of being unconscious. We have become so accustomed to numbing our senses that that is all we seek to do in our free time. Toxins are what we crave.

From the food that we eat to the drugs we consume to the music we listen to, much of it is garbage lacking substance or essence. When we look at the music industry, for example, much of it is mechanically manufactured and lacks any real artistic virtue. Not so long ago the real art of music was expressed. Musicians were real artists, where they all wrote their own music and lyrics that reflected the life they lived. It had a story to tell.

When art is a reflection of nature, meaning what is within the human being, then it has the power to change the world. But in general, because of our addiction to the dope, we have lost connection with our artistic nature. What is popular in the music industry today is really only pop music—and let's be frank: pop musicians are increasingly groomed by reality TV shows promising future stardom. Music has become secondary to fame for its own sake, and so music today is devoid of art, and therefore devoid of any real musicians. This empty pop is the music we all know too well, constantly and repetitively played on radios and television, infiltrating our subconscious so you hypnotically purchase the album or single. We find ourselves unconsciously tapping our feet to catchy beats and, frankly, poor music.

But pop music is not actually a new problem. In the Warring States period of China Confucius addressed people's addiction to the dope as well. Pop music was a detriment to real art in Confucius's time. In the *Analects,* the text attributed to Confucius, he highlights the unconscious attraction people have toward the distractions of the dope of pop music. The type of music he criticized was that of the Zheng vassal state in China during the Zhou dynasty and he described those attracted to this sort of music as *glib.* In the *Analects* Confucius explains this to Yan Hui in response to his inquiry about running a state:

Follow the calendar of the Xia, travel in the carriages of the Shang, and clothe yourself in the ceremonial caps of the Zhou.

As for music, listen only to the Shao and Wu. Prohibit the tunes of Zheng, and keep glib people at a distance—for the tunes of Zheng are licentious, and glib people are dangerous.[5]

To explain this more clearly, American professor of Asian studies at the University of British Columbia Edward Slingerland states in his commentary to his translation on the *Analects*:

The Shao and Wu represent the best of classical, properly formed music, in contrast to the licentious, seductive popular music of Zheng that was the rage among Confucius' contemporaries. The lyrics of the Zheng music were somewhat racy, and although little is known about the exact nature of the music, commentators assert that it had a simple but catchy beat, was sung by mixed groups of men and women, and gave rise to sexual improprieties—all of which should sound very familiar to concerned parents of any nation or age.[6]

Confucius points out that it is not always natural to be lost in the moment, or to be swayed by the rhythm. That is, if the mind is driven by external distractions then it is only responding to agitation. We could say this perception suits Confucius's conservative temperament, but he definitely does make a point.

A mind that has fasted can be truly awake and enjoy life from a place within ourselves that is not dependent on external circumstances. Real joy arises from within and is not momentary, but the joy we believe we are experiencing in the outside world is always momentary. When we are truly experiencing the beauty of art, for example, our body does not unconsciously move to the rhythm of the impressions of the external world (unless you are actually performing the art of dance and are a skilled dancer trained to move with the rhythm as an art form rather than someone who is disconnected from the art). On the contrary, when the mind has fasted, there are no more distractions between mind and body and we are ever present to experience the beauty of art from the joy of stillness. We are completely present to appreciate it fully.

In the classic original philosophy of yoga brought to life by the great Indian sage Patanjali (not the popular fitness craze masquerading as yoga), he states that the elegance of *prakrti* (all the form and energy of the manifest universe, including thoughts) is divine only when we perceive it from the pure awareness of our true nature—Purusha, that is, absolute pure awareness and the identical source of the universe within each of us, similar to the concept of Atman in Vedic scripture. Otherwise, prakrti is just a tornado of distraction in which the mind becomes lost. If we do not fulfill the purpose of life to realize Purusha as our original nature, then we will continually be asleep because we are doped out of our mind. To awaken from this sleep we need to check ourselves into the rehabilitation clinic of mind fasting. To understand how we fast the mind we need to first understand its origins, science, lifestyle, and practice.

3
CULTURAL AND HISTORICAL BACKGROUND

The origins of mind fasting go way back to ancient Asia, especially China and the Indian subcontinent. According to the evidence available, both cultures gave birth to the practice of fasting the mind at almost identical times in history. Actually, when we examine both cultures centuries before the Common Era there are numerous similarities, especially in the sociological systems of the Hindu caste system and Confucianism. Whether they result from the collective unconscious or the sharing of ideas at that time, the similarities are nevertheless remarkable. In regard to fasting the mind, both cultures gave birth to this practice in response to the same social and spiritual problems that plagued the common thought of their era.

THE VEDIC CIVILIZATION

The Vedic civilization was born in the Indus Valley region, which is an area that extends from northeast Afghanistan to Pakistan and northwest India. It existed from 1500 to 500 BCE. This rich spiritual culture is still alive today in India through Hinduism. The Vedic civilization came to exist through the mixing of two different peoples and cultures. The ancient Dravidian people were the original inhabitants of the Indus Valley from about 2500 to 1500 BCE (some scholars suggest that this culture may have been even more ancient). Then around 1500 BCE the Aryan people came sweeping in from the north and invaded the Dravidian civilization. Out of this reluctant marriage came the rich culture we know as the Vedic civilization. This one civilization has influenced the world like no other. From the religions and philosophies we have, both Eastern and Western, to the moral and ethical systems we have in place for societies, the Vedic culture is a key driving force of thought.

At the inception of the Vedic culture, the Aryan people dominated the Dravidians. When the social system of the Hindu castes came into being, the top two castes were Aryans and the lower two were Dravidians. The Hindu caste system is made up of the Brahmins (magician priests/scholars/priest class), Kshatriyas (nobility/warrior class), Vaishyas (merchants and farmers), and Shudras (laborers/peasants). The Aryans occupied the castes of the Brahmins and Kshatriyas. From that position of power the Aryans could influence the whole civilization with their own spiritual and political views. Yet from the outset the spiritual and political views of the Aryans were subtly influenced by the Dravidians.

Over the duration of this reluctant marriage of cultures a more ancient mystical tradition began to reveal itself. This was a mysticism and spirituality that was part of the pre-Aryan Dravidian civilization. It was almost lost in the merging of two cultures, but its essential essence has an enduring quality. The Aryan Brahmins were not aware of this mystical tradition of the Dravidians because their primary (possibly only) spiritual practice was ritual sacrifice. But even their sacrificial ritual was influenced in part by the Dravidians. They developed a series of sacred hymns to coincide with the magic and mystery of their rituals, which became the sacred texts of the Vedas. Before the Aryans formulated the Vedas into hymns and texts, they had been part of a mysterious oral tradition among the Dravidian people, which were preserved through elaborate mnemonic techniques (known in Sanskrit as *dharani,* which is a term for a type of ritual speech similar to a mantra) that somehow contain an immense power. This subtle influence of the Dravidian oral tradition within the Aryan sacrificial ritual gave the Aryans awareness of this power, an energy they felt even in their rituals before the sacred hymns but even more present with them. This power, or universal energy, was called Brahman in Sanskrit.

The Aryan Brahmins thought that this universal energy, or irreducible essence, of Brahman could be evoked only during sacrificial ritual. They could feel the presence of Brahman during those rites, but it was only momentary, which made them think that Brahman was separate from the ordinary world.

BIRTH OF THE VANAPRASTHA

In these rites were where the more ancient knowledge, wisdom, and mysticism of Brahman from the Dravidian culture began to resurface. Some of the Aryan Brahmin priests began to feel the presence of Brahman in their hearts and in the ordinary world all the time, even outside of rituals. Feeling Brahman in all aspects of life and within their hearts, some of the priests had a trust or faith that was unwavering, and they began to walk the Earth and contemplate the essence of the universe. The prolific English writer, novelist, and philosopher Aldous Huxley alluded to this in his anthology *The Perennial Philosophy*:

> We have seen that, when they are promoted to be the central core of organized religious worship, ritualism and sacramentalism are by no means unmixed blessings. But that the whole of a man's workaday life should be transformed by him into a kind of continuous ritual, that every object in the world around him should be regarded as a symbol of the world's eternal Ground, that all his actions should

be performed sacramentally this would seem to be wholly desirable. All the masters of the spiritual life, from the authors of the Upanishads to Socrates, from Buddha to St. Bernard, are agreed that without self-knowledge there cannot be adequate knowledge of God, that without a constant recollectedness there can be no complete deliverance.[1]

This sense of the divine within the ordinary world was the birth of the *vanaprastha,* a forest sage or philosopher who has broken away from caste and society. In my book *Enlightenment Now* I explain the significance of the arrival of the vanaprastha in the Vedic civilization and how they were the most crucial element in the revival of the ancient mystical Dravidian tradition of contemplation and individual self-work. The vanaprastha were forest philosophers who came to understand that the energy of ritual sacrifice was actually present in all of life. This meant that sacrificial rituals weren't actually necessary to realize Brahman. Rather, it could be attained through self-work, that is, inner contemplation.

The vanaprastha became an integral part of the Hindu caste system, as eventually there was an option to leave society for good around the age of forty-five, once all of our household and family duties were fulfilled. The vanaprastha were the original renouncers of the world. This renunciant temperament probably existed in the Dravidian culture prior to the Aryan invasion.

When the vanaprastha leaves society they have the option to return to society or to renounce society until death. The latter option is the preferred choice because the idea is that we give our life over so completely to Brahman that all attachments to the physical and mental sphere of the universe (prakrti) are extinguished. This is true, but this is not the highest realization of the vanaprastha. What they eventually realized is that you don't need to renounce the physical and mental worlds, but instead you need to renounce the content and distractions of your mind that keep you separate and isolated from Brahman.

THE PHILOSOPHY AND PRACTICE
OF *NETI NETI*

The vanaprastha began to return to society with a completely different perception of the world. This new vision arose from the process of mental renunciation, the original mind fasting. They realized we do not need to leave society, but instead we need to refrain from the conditioning we have acquired from the world. When we fast the mind like this we develop resonance with Brahman, so it doesn't matter where you physically are in the world because you are always home.

The core method, then, for realizing the ultimate reality (Brahman) is mental renunciation, which I call mind fasting. As a result of this wisdom, we have the birth of probably the most significant texts to come out of India, and maybe the world, known as the Upanishads. The Upanishads give the first evidence of mind fasting through its philosophy and practice of *neti neti,* which in Sanskrit means "neither this nor that" or "not this, not this."

In the *Brihadaranyaka Upanishad* from 700 BCE there is an emphasis on understanding that Atman (the true self, the deep-down, real you with no mental content or attachment to the physical world) is Brahman (ultimate reality), meaning that the idea of separateness in the world is born only from believing each of us is a permanent individual with a lasting personality. This illusion of a personal and permanent soul is known as the *jiva* or *jivatman* in Sanskrit. Jiva is the reflection of Brahman in ignorance, the illusion of *maya,* which is a Sanskrit term referring to the measurement of reality into isolated separate parts. To realize we are Atman and not the idea of who we think we are on a personal level (jiva), the philosophy and practice of neti neti came to fruition. The practice of this mental negation is supposed to transform your consciousness by not associating your mind with anything and also through realizing that everything and everyone you see is also Atman, whether they know it or not is not your problem, because in the end you see only Brahman. The *Brihadaranyaka Upanishad* states:

About this (atman), one can only say "not—, not—." He is ungrasp-able, for he cannot be grasped. He is undecaying, for he is not sub-ject to decay. He has nothing sticking to him, for he does not stick to anything. He is not bound; yet he neither trembles in fear nor suffers injury.[2]

In modern times a lot of spiritual teachers misinterpret neti neti in the same way that the original vanaptrasthas thought we need to literally renounce the physical world. Neti neti can be misunderstood to relate to the negation of the body and physical world, rather than the renunciation of the mental content, habits, and activity that make up our temporary persona. One might also conclude that we are not the physical body, and while this is true eternally, for the time being if you are reading these words then you know you have a body. In truth, it is not the body that is the problem but the overidentification with it, which actually arises from the mind. The poor old body becomes the innocent victim to our ego and our attempts to transcend the ego, which in truth is itself an egotistical attempt. Leave the poor body alone; you were given it against your will and it is a gift because only in this body can you experience the divine supreme reality. The real renunciation is not physical but rather is the renunciation of the content within your mind. As the great sage and mind-fasting practitioner Sri Ramana Maharshi once said:

Renunciation is always in the mind, not in going to forests or soli-tary places or giving up one's duties. The main thing is to see that the mind does not turn outward but inward. It does not really rest with a man whether he goes to this place or that or whether he gives up his duties or not. All these events happen according to destiny. All the activities that the body is to go through are determined when it first comes into existence. It does not rest with you to accept or reject them. The only freedom you have is to turn your mind inward and renounce activities there.[3]

The "neither this nor that" of neti neti is referring to the ability to reside in your true nature of pure awareness (Purusha) and perceive the rising thoughts and tendencies that drive our beliefs and opinions without attachment or identification with them. This heightened level of discrimination and discernment within our mind is known as *viveka* in Sanskrit. In the practice of viveka, which encompasses Purusha's witnessing of prakrti's mental fluctuations, you are developing the natural state of being an objective witness to the ever-moving content in your mind. Inadvertently, whether you know it or not, the more you do this the more you begin to reside in the original nondual nature of Purusha. The more you reside in Purusha, or Atman, the less power your mental activity has over you. Actually, the frequency of thoughts, feelings, and emotions begins to diminish as your internal landscape becomes increasingly quiet. This quiet mind, absorbed in Brahman, is your original nature. This is the mind that has completely fasted.

Neti neti is a method to deliver us from the illusion of reality, which is the tendency to name, like, and dislike things according to your conditioning and mental activity. The Sanskrit word for this illusion is *maya,* as we briefly mentioned earlier. Maya is often misunderstood as the concept that reality is not solid or permanent because it is made up of atoms and even subatomic particles, most of which are actually empty space. The science here might be right but this is not the original Vedic concept of maya, even though they did know about atoms without the advent of modern science. *Maya* comes from the Sanskrit root *matr,* which means measurement. This is also the root of the Greco-Latin words *matter, meter,* and *matrix,* all of which pertain to measuring. The original concept of the illusionary measurement of maya is when we begin to dissect reality according to our conditioning and mental activity. Measuring life according to our own conditioned personality. As we all know too well, the more we cut reality up like this the more we suffer as a result of this tendency.

To get out of this illusion of maya we need to practice viveka and neti neti, which is the cure that I call fasting the mind. Through fasting the mind, the vanaprastha realized their reflection in the eternal still waters of Brahman once the turbulence of the waves and ripples of their mind had settled. Once they had settled and the vanaprastha looked into their own nature, they could see that consciousness is naturally transparent and reflective from their empty, still, and pure mind.

This same knowledge also arose around the same time in Chinese culture with the great Taoist sage Chuang-tzu.

HUNDRED SCHOOLS OF THOUGHT IN ANCIENT CHINA

The classical period of Chinese philosophy known as the Hundred Schools of Thought (諸子百家) flourished from the sixth century to 221 BCE, during the Spring and Autumn period of the Warring States period of ancient China. The Hundred Schools of Thought produced some of the more influential figures that still reverberate in our consciousness today. At the beginning of that period we have the founder of Taoism, Lao-tzu, believed to have been born around 571 BCE, and Confucius (551–479 BCE) the founder of Confucianism.* Coming after both of these great sages we have a chain of great philosophers who contributed to both Chinese philosophies. In historical order we have Mo-tzu (470–391 BCE), Mencius (372–289 BCE), Chuang-tzu (circa 369–286 BCE), and Hsun-tzu (circa 313–238 BCE). These later thinkers elaborated on and contributed to the teachings of both Lao-tzu and

---

*Taoism is a spiritual and philosophical tradition that focuses on living in harmony with the Tao, literally "the Way" or "way of nature." This requires one to live in harmony with the course of nature, mimicking its functions, its simplicity, and its spontaneity, which give us the sense of naturalness in our lives. There is an emphasis on letting nature run its course in Taoism as opposed to other religious traditions, which assume we need to adhere to rituals and ceremonies. Taoism asserts that we are nature and so the Tao is already within the world. Confucianism is a socioeconomic-political-religious ideology based on the teachings of Confucius that runs counter to Taoism, as Confucianism is based on creating virtuous people through a moral and ethical system that is supposed to induce the Tao in the world. This implies that Confucius believes we need to be molded rather than letting nature run its course.

Confucius. Some took a hard-line stance for one or the other, such as Hsun-tzu's attachment to Confucianism, while others took the good parts of both philosophies, such as Mencius, whose thinking was Taoist even though he called himself a Confucian.

Both the philosophies of Taoist and Confucian thought have been influential in the evolution of Chinese culture. Yet they stand at opposite ends of how they view the world. For example, Confucianism is a socioeconomic-political-religious system that is supposed to shape the individual according to the four basic virtues of Confucius, a philosophy known as *Ju* (儒). The four virtues are: *jen* (仁), human heartedness, the compassion and devotional love we have deep down for one another, the ability to identify with the suffering and joy of others as if they were our own; *yi* (義), a sense of justice, responsibility, duty and obligation to others; *li* (禮, not to be confused with its homophone, 理) acting out of love and veneration for relationships; and *chih* (智), wisdom, the embodiment of the three other virtues into a spiritual maturity, where we follow our spontaneous inner obedience toward the Tao rather than being moved by external influences.

This system is supposed to get the individual out of egocentric self-interest and into a more selfless role that will contribute to the society rather than our own desires, needs, and interests. If we are to follow this method then the *Tao* (translated as the Way, it refers to the irreducible essence of the universe, which is the same as the Brahman of Indian philosophy) enters our life and society, bringing the world into resonance with that divine principle. By following our social duty (social dharma) according to Confucianism, we are supposed to be in harmony with the Tao because we have curbed our latent desires on an individual level and surrendered to what is needed for the greater society.

The problem with this suppression of latent desires, as we have witnessed through the course of history, is they persist and become an inhibitor to an individual's psychological growth if they continue to be suppressed. This doesn't mean that we become egotistically self-interested; instead it means that deep within us we have a unique gift to share with the world that will inadvertently bring harmony to the world. There are two Chinese concepts to articulate this; the first is *li* (理), which translated literally originally referred to the markings in jade and muscle fibers. The Chinese always have interesting and poetic ways to describe things, especially their inner natures. In relation to philosophy *li* refers to an organic pattern of the universe.

This organic pattern is within us as our own unique, latent, psychological, and creative interests. We come into resonance with this pattern only when our mind is empty. This is how a sage speaks divine truth, and artists express divine beauty—because they have shut down their ordinary conscious mind and allowed the Tao to move through them. This is the Chinese concept of *wu-wei* (無爲), which is translated as effortless action, nondoing, and ultimately the psychological ability of applying no force.

The second Chinese concept that li leads to is *ying* (應), a word meaning "mutual resonance and interdependence." This means that by following your organic pattern you bring harmony to the world because this is how the function of the Tao operates and manifests. This is where conjecture over the use and meaning of the Sanskrit word *dharma* arises. *Dharma* is an inclusive word that can mean "duty," "mission," "the Buddha's teaching," or "virtue." When we take the word to mean duty, that implies people following the needs of the society, which, frankly, are the needs of political leaders. But when we take *dharma* to mean "virtue," we see that we are virtuous and life itself is virtuous, making none of us more special than anybody else. In an empty mind we become conscious of this dharma as it is experienced as an intense will, and is thought of in the East as the Divine will of the universe. By following this virtuous power within we ignite our li and in doing so we bring ying to the world.

The Chinese equivalent to dharma is *te* (德) and it is all about this virtue we become conscious of within. This word *te* has a special meaning in Taoism. It is part of the title of the classic Taoist text, the *Tao Te Ching,* which means "The Way and Its Virtue" or "The Way and

Its Power." Both interpretations mean that the Tao is naturally virtuous and this virtue functions through us when our mind is empty, and it is revealed in the power it emanates through such an empty mind. The Taoist approach to recognizing the Tao is diametrically opposed to Confucian thought, which brings us to the Taoist thought of China.

Lao-tzu's approach to life and understanding the universe is natural and organic, as opposed to the Confucian perspective of structure and discipline. While there is discipline in original Taoist thought, it is linked more to a dedication to a simple lifestyle and the art of living it. The view of original Taoism is that the universe is grown organically rather than and not something created by some sort of creator, such as God, for example. Taoism is a natural approach, and always concerned with how nature primarily *is*. In Taoist thought nature is silent, empty of a separate mind, beautiful, simple, and devoid of intellectual meaning. Lao-tzu advocated that the Tao is in all life and is felt in our experience when our mind has returned to its original nature, empty, silent, simple, and so on. The idea that the Tao could be found by following a social system like Confucianism was absurd to Lao-tzu. This is evident in an imaginary dialogue between Lao-tzu and Confucius imagined by Chuang-tzu:

Figure 3.1. Confucius and Lao-tzu in dialogue.
By Jiwon Kim (Lathandar).

"Tell me," said Lao-tzu, "in what consist charity and duty to one's neighbour?"

"They consist," answered Confucius, "in a capacity for rejoicing in all things; in universal love, without the element of self. These are the characteristics of charity and duty to one's neighbour."

"What stuff!" cried Lao-tzu. "Does not universal love contradict itself? Is not your elimination of self a positive manifestation of self? Sir, if you would cause the empire not to lose its source of nourishment—there is the universe, its regularity is unceasing; there are the sun and moon, their brightness is unceasing; there are the stars, their groupings never change; there are the birds and beasts, they flock together without varying; there are the trees and shrubs, they grow upwards without exception. Be like these: follow Tao, and you will be perfect. Why then these vain struggles after charity and duty to one's neighbour, as though beating a drum in search of a fugitive. Alas! Sir, you have brought much confusion into the mind of man."[4]

If there is an irreducible essence in all life naturally throughout the universe, then it is absurd to think we can bring that irreducible essence into the world or to have erroneous beliefs that it is separate and in some more absurd cases that it is a separate "being" from us as our ruler. The simplicity and emptiness of nature is the Way of the Tao, the presence of Brahman, and we are that nature. Yet in defense of Confucianism and the Hindu caste system, they were not entirely incorrect in their way of thinking. They could both be thought of as spiritual systems for our mind, because in following either system we have to surrender to something greater than ourselves, which naturally makes us less egocentric and self-interested, a spiritual goal indeed. Though this is true, the problem with this thinking is the Tao and Brahman are thought to be separate from life, which leads to erroneous ideas of a monarchical universe because we begin to think of ourselves in relation to the Tao, Brahman, God, or the universe as subject to a king or lord.

These types of similarities between the Vedic civilization of the Indian subcontinent and the Hundred Schools of Thought period of China are uncanny. The Hindu caste system and Confucianism are almost identical in their approach of trying to bring the divine energy of the universe into life. The Brahmins thought Brahman existed only in ritual sacrifice and in reciting the sacred hymns, while the Confucians thought the Tao came into life by following the Four Books and Five Classics of Confucian thought, including rituals and sacrifices that are supposed to evoke the four basic virtues of Confucianism and make us a *chun-tzu* (superior man). In response and almost identical is the knowledge and wisdom of the vanaprastha and Lao-tzu. It is amazing that both philosophies realize that the eternal essence of the universe is not a long time away, but actually that it is right *now* where thinking and time cease. The vanaprastha and early Taoists left the social constraints of the physical and mental world to realize this truth. But there was one great Taoist who replicated the vanaprastha's return to the world with the wisdom of mind fasting that we previously only found in the Upanishads.

CHUANG-TZU:
IN THE WORLD BUT NOT OF IT

The teaching and wisdom of fasting the mind is found in the classic Taoist text known as the *Chuang-tzu*, which is believed to be authored by the great sage Chuang-tzu. Chuang-tzu is the second-best-known Taoist sage after Lao-tzu. (There is, however, more evidence that Chuang-tzu was a real person, whereas Lao-tzu was most likely a mythological figure.) Chuang-tzu lived toward the end of the Warring States period of China, from 369 to 286 BCE, so he had the vantage point of coming after so many great philosophers of those times. He had the opportunity to contemplate and reflect upon the differences between Taoist and Confucian thought that occupied philosophers of that time. In doing so, Chuang-tzu could bring clarity to the matter like no other.

In some sense he went against a lot of Taoists who believed, as did the original vanaprastha, that to realize the Tao/Brahman we need to leave the physical confines of society. Chuang-tzu symbolizes the return of the vanaprastha to society, "bringing back the boon," to use Joseph Campbell's words. This return has nothing to do with the Buddhist bodhisattva ideal of returning to the world to liberate all beings from suffering, though this may inadvertently be the result. But instead it is more to do with the realization that the Tao is everywhere and within everything, much the same as the mythological story of the Mahayana Buddhists when they got on a ferryboat to leave this world and embark to the yonder shore of the world of *nirvana*. And yet, when they arrived at the yonder shore they realized they had been in the world of nirvana all the time, they just couldn't perceive it through their polluted minds.

When Chuang-tzu realized the Tao in his everyday experience, he recognized that it was the habits, tendencies, and conditioning of our society and culture that eclipse this awareness. Chuang-tzu understood that it was not the society and culture itself that ought to be demonized, but instead the motives that drive them. In the American scholar and translator Burton Watson's introduction to *The Complete Works of Chuang-tzu* he states:

> In Chuang Tzu's view, the man who has freed himself from conventional standards of judgment can no longer be made to suffer, for he refuses to recognize poverty as any less desirable then affluence, to recognize death as any less desirable than life. He does not in any literal sense withdraw and hide from the world—to do so would show that he still passed judgment upon the world. He remains within society but refrains from acting out of the motives that lead ordinary men to struggle for wealth, fame, success, or safety. He maintains a state that Chuang Tzu refers to as *wu-wei*, or inaction, meaning by this term not a forced quietude, but a course of action that is not founded upon any purposeful motives of gain or striving. In such a state, all human actions become as spontaneous and mindless

as those of the natural world. Man becomes one with Nature, or Heaven, as Chuang Tzu calls it, and merges himself with Tao, or the Way, the underlying unity that embraces man, Nature, and all that is in the universe.

To describe this mindless, purposeless mode of life, Chuang Tzu turns most often to the analogy of the artist or craftsman. The skilled woodcarver, the skilled butcher, the skilled swimmer does not ponder or ratiocinate on the course of action he should take; his skill has become so much a part of him that he merely acts instinctively and spontaneously and, without knowing why, achieves success. Again, Chuang Tzu employs the metaphor of a totally free and purposeless journey, using the word *yu* (to wander, or a wandering) to designate the way in which the enlightened man wanders through all of creation, enjoying its delights without ever becoming attached to any one part of it.[5]

The problem he identified was that social and cultural conditioning is so deep that people in general find it hard to resist the temptations the world offers. Chuang-tzu realized that ordinary meditation methods could not help alleviate this conditioning. Our lifestyle needed to change fundamentally. In the same way that the Vedic people realized this so did Chuang-tzu, maybe because of his own insight, the collective unconscious, or the supposed arrival of the Zen master Bodhidharma from India to China. Nevertheless, Chuang-tzu came to know a philosophy that was only known previously in the Upanishads and maybe Dravidian culture pre-Aryan. This is the sacred healing method of fasting the mind. The phrase *fasting the mind* is actually first found in the *Chuang-tzu*, though its practice is much older.

The teaching of fasting the mind appears in the *Chuang-tzu* through a story about how to change a corrupt ruler's nature. In the story Confucius plays Chuang-tzu's mouthpiece and is the sage figure. (In general Chuang-tzu would not be in favor of Confucius and his teachings, but in this story Chuang-tzu uses him as the sage because he was the most well-known figure of China in those ancient times.) Chuang-tzu's Confucius has a disciple in the story called Yen Hui. Yen Hui hears of a ruler in the state of Wei in China who treats the common people poorly, so Yen Hui seeks to change the ruler's character so that it becomes virtuous like that of a sage.

Yen Hui explains to Confucius that he will be traveling to Wei with a calculated strategy for changing the young ruler. His strategy is based on the words of Confucius, which he believes are the standard for restoring health to the state of Wei. Confucius refutes such a strategy and explains to Yen Hui that he will probably get himself executed with such ambitious actions. Confucius is blunt in pointing out that only a "perfect man" of ancient times who knew within himself the Tao could consider passing on his knowledge and wisdom to others because his mind would not be mixed up with the troubles of the world. But even then, as Confucius points out, the perfect man is cautious and invariably doesn't share wisdom with people who do not ask for it. This is because the perfect man follows the Tao, and if someone doesn't ask then that means they are not ready to hear the truth. This is the way of nature, the way of no force.

In this passage in the *Chuang-tzu* Confucius explains that those people who seek to change the world without truly knowing the Way destroy virtue and their wisdom becomes a device for "wrangling." Confucius explains to Yen Hui that if he doesn't know the minds of others and uses his fame to deliver sermons on benevolence and righteousness to a ruler, then all he will actually do is use people's faults to parade his own so-called wisdom. This is spiritual pride, and it is why Confucius is concerned for Yen Hui's well-being.

Nevertheless, Yen Hui continues to explain a number of different strategies for changing the young ruler, but Confucius shows him how each one is flawed and will end in disaster. It appears Yen Hui has thought of everything, but still he does not satisfy the master. Yen Hui has left out the essential practice of mind fasting in all strategies that doesn't please Confucius at all. Actually by the time Yen Hui has explained all of his glamorous strategies Confucius is fed up and has heard enough:

> Confucius said, "Goodness, how could that do? You have too many policies and plans and you haven't seen what is needed. You will probably get off without incurring any blame, yes. But that will be as far as it goes. How do you think you can actually convert him? You are still making the mind your teacher!"
>
> Yen Hui said, "I have nothing more to offer. May I ask the proper way?"
>
> "You must fast!" said Confucius. "I will tell you what that means. Do you think it is easy to do anything while you have [a mind]? If you do, Bright Heaven will not sanction you."
>
> Yen Hui said, "My family is poor. I haven't drunk wine or eaten any strong foods for several months. So can I be considered as having fasted?"
>
> "That is the fasting one does before a sacrifice, not the fasting of the mind."
>
> "May I ask what the fasting of the mind is?"
>
> Confucius said, "Make your will one! Don't listen with your ears, listen with your mind. No, don't listen with your mind, but listen with your spirit. Listening stops with the ears, the mind stops with recognition, but spirit is empty and waits on all things. The Way gathers in emptiness alone. Emptiness is the fasting of the mind."
>
> Yen Hui said, "Before I heard this, I was certain that I was Hui. But now that I have heard it, there is no more Hui. Can this be called emptiness?"
>
> "That's all there is to it," said Confucius. "Now I will tell you. You may go and play in his bird cage, but never be moved by fame. If he listens, then sing; if not, keep still. Have no gate, no opening, but make oneness your house and live with what cannot be avoided. Then you will be close to success."[6]

In this passage we find that Confucius shoots down all of Yen Hui's attempts at trying to intentionally change the ruler according to his own will. Instead, Confucius advocates that Yen Hui should fast his mind because he is still making the mind his ruler. Yen Hui is not allowing life to happen as it will in true Taoist fashion. His own personal agendas are still interfering with the universal flow of Tao. Only when Yen Hui's sense of himself—meaning the sense of "I," the conscious mind or ego—dissolves can he truly change things, because then the Tao will have taken over him.

The Tao gravitates toward that which is empty. This is exactly the same as dharma (virtue) in Hindu philosophy, meaning the Divine will shine only through those who have relinquished their own personal will or even insightfully recognized that there is no such thing as an individual will, thus there is only one will: Brahman. As I mentioned earlier, Taoists explain this emptiness through questions like "What is more valuable: the cup or the space within the cup?" This is a metaphor about our mind and the space we create for divine will to be recognized. We don't often value the empty space within our mind because we rush around to fill it up with useless noise. That's why it is so important to fast the mind and get back to your original nature of emptiness, where the divine presence of the universe moves through you. The charade of you being this person with all of these dramas has ceased and the pure awareness of Purusha becomes your center of gravity, because that is your real center of gravity. We have just lost sight of that through the fog of our mind. Mind fasting is the ray of sunshine that penetrates deeply into this fog until it is entirely evaporated.

This method has no particular character that belongs to any certain culture. We discover this in how the idea of mind fasting came about in two separate parts of the world. We see this in the story of Yen Hui, as he explored the same kind of neti neti wisdom described in the Upanishads and allowed the mind-fasting rays of sunshine evaporate his identity of being a separate entity.

But the similarities between the Upanishads and Chuang-tzu do not stop with mind fasting.

Chuang-tzu had his own philosophy similar to neti neti with its components of viveka and maya. Yet he went about it in a different manner. Chuang-tzu realized that we have this ability to discriminate between this and that in our mind. He believed that this ability to discern and measure reality (that is, maya) is a human flaw. In the *Chuang-tzu* he uses the word *qing* (情), which can mean "facts, emotions, or specie-specific essence." In regard to the *Chuang-tzu*, *qing* means "specific essence."

This interpretation of qing is drawn from Mohist logical theory.* Qing is what makes a horse gallop gracefully like no other and a cobra stand up and hiss like no other, for example. But Chuang-tzu believes that human qing is flawed because when we discern between this and that in our mind it leads ultimately to subjective opinions of right and wrong, good and evil, likes and dislikes, and so on. This is the illusion of maya: the illusion of functioning according to qing actually causes so many problems in the world. As a result, Chuang-tzu and the great sages of the past realized the dire need for fasting the mind. When we fast the mind, we lose qing. Qing gives birth to the sense of the separate and isolated "I" we think we are. A sage loses this human flaw by fasting the mind and then begins to move in accord and in harmony with the Tao, as Chuang-tzu explains:

> The sage has the outward physical appearance of a human being but lacks human essence. Because he looks like a human, he flocks together with other people. Lacking human essence, though, he does not allow right or wrong to get to him. Lowly! Small! In this way he belongs to the world of humans. Elevated! Great! Standing alone, he perfects his Heavenly qualities.[7]

---

*Mohist logical theory is part of Mohism. Mohism was an ancient Chinese philosophy during the Warring States period based on logic, rational thought, and science developed by academic scholars who studied under the ancient Chinese philosopher Mo-tzu.

The problem for us mere mortals is how to live authentically from this original nature that fasting the mind evokes. How do we understand all of this knowledge and wisdom from our history and become modern sages? First we need to realize that it is not something you can attain overnight. Mind fasting is a science that is applied to your consciousness and that throws your current life upside down. The original science of mind fasting is ancient but eternal, and, more important, it is relevant to your life today.

4

THE ANCIENT
SCIENCE OF
MIND FASTING

Fasting the mind was born in response to a world with its attention fixed on outside phenomena, which we relate to through our conditioning. The practice of mind fasting is a scientific inquiry of the internal landscape of our body and mind. As we mentioned in the previous chapter, it came about in response to a world with its mind oriented toward externalization through the process of reacting to the mind's activity and movement. When people hear this they think it is as simple as refraining from their mental habits and ignoring their emotional responses to the external world. Though both of these will help, the science of mind fasting is much more subtle and it requires thorough understanding.

If we don't understand it thoroughly we run the risk of falling into misinterpretation while we still seek egotistical ends, in this case trying to become enlightened as if it is your personality that attains it. We see this trap in the modern yoga movement, in which people think yoga is a physical exercise for health and well-being. Few people understand that what they do in the gym is related only to hatha yoga, but it is not true yoga because it has been stripped of the philosophy and psychology of yoga, which must be understood and lived if you are to practice one of the numerous branches of yoga authentically. I don't want you to fall into this trap when you begin to practice fasting the mind. I want you to come to this science with no preconceptions and an empty mind, with a sincerity and keen desire to know your true nature. Only then can you begin to apply this science to your everyday life.

The ancient science of mind fasting was discovered by the great explorers of consciousness, great mystics including the original Vanaprasthas, Gautama the Buddha, Chuang-tzu, even Patanjali, the founder of classical yoga. They traversed the depths of the mind and returned with a science that promises everlasting liberation and the end of suffering. Only a few people ever find this science, so I congratulate you if you are reading these words: you are here because you yearn for true freedom.

After traversing the depths of consciousness, the great mystics came back with a science to share with the world. But this science cannot be examined in a regular scientific laboratory because the laboratory is actually the mind. The science of fasting the mind requires you to thoroughly examine your mind at all times. In doing so, you gain a better understanding of your subconscious content and how it drives unconscious actions. Experimenting in the laboratory of the mind can be painful, and you could easily fall back into old habits to try and escape from facing yourself, because in fasting the mind you yourself are both the subject and object of examination. In ancient times, and still now, people at first find it uncomfortable to be constantly in the laboratory of the mind while functioning among people who are still asleep to their true nature, hypnotized by physical and mental distractions. As a result, the ancient scientists of the mind set up healthy environments to facilitate a thorough examination of the mind.

THE ANCIENT MIND FASTING CLINICS

The great sages of history, going way back to the Upanishads, understood that fasting the mind is an essential teaching in order to "know thyself." This knowledge from the Upanishads and the Vedas became the science and philosophy of Vedanta, which is one of the core philosophies of Hinduism. When the teaching of Vedanta began to spread to the common people, the main idea of its philosophy was the same as within the Upanishads: nondualism, which in Sanskrit is known as *advaita*. The attainment of advaita awareness and perception is the eventual outcome of fasting the mind. Classically known as Advaita Vedanta, it is a spiritual science that aspires to evoke within your consciousness the great wisdom of the Upanishads that Atman is Brahman. This is why the great advaita master Sri Ramana Maharshi said:

> So the fact is that *Brahman* is all and remains indivisible. It is ever realised but man is not aware of this. He must come to know this. Knowledge means the overcoming of obstacles which obstruct the revelation of the eternal truth that the Self is the same as *Brahman*. The obstacles taken together form your idea of separateness as an individual.
>
> The ancients say: "Making the vision absorbed in *jnana* one sees the world as *Brahman*."[1]

In Jnana Yoga (that is, "Yoga of Wisdom"), one who perceives the world as Brahman is referred to by the honorable title of *jnani*. Jnana Yoga is considered the advanced path of yoga practiced by great sages because it is only for those who recognize Brahman rather than the duality of maya. A jnani, then, is a great seer of the divine. From fasting the mind their consciousness has been purged of the illusion of separation. The toxic, distracted mind cannot perceive this divine reality. It is lost in the separateness of maya's illusionary distractions. One such jnani, Shankara (788–820 CE), the great Indian philosopher of Vedic thought, articulates this better:

Brahman is real,
the universe is unreal, and
The universe is Brahman.[2]

This stanza may appear contradictory, but it truly is not. The last line explains the first two: the world is unreal when we perceive it as a reality composed of separate parts. However, the universe is real only when we perceive it as Brahman, because reality itself is actually nondual. To acquire the perception of jnanis such as Sri Ramana Maharshi and Shankara, and to live the wisdom of the Upanishads, the first known spiritual clinics were set up. These were known as *ashrams* in Sanskrit. An ashram is a spiritual retreat where we can stay to be close to a master who embodies advaita as a living reality. Ashrams are intentionally designed very simply, with no outside distractions, where you are in the presence of the master at all times. This master holds *satsangs* (discussions of truth) every day and enforces a strict discipline and regime to follow. Ashrams these days follow the same formula as set out by the ancients, though there are increasingly nowadays ashrams that diverge from this tradition.

The evolution of Upanishadic spirituality led to probably one of the best-known spiritual clinics and teachers the world has known, Buddhism and Gautama the Buddha, respectively. The original teaching of Gautama the Buddha is known as vipassana, insight into your true nature and is an extended teaching and science of the earlier Upanishadic tradition. Buddhism itself is not truthfully a religion; it should be thought of as "the science of mind." This science is the practice of vipassana (continuous insight into your true nature) in every moment to realize the same end as Advaita Vedanta, though the interpretation and semantics of this attainment are different. But the experience is the same. The teachings of Buddha (*dhamma* in Pali or *dharma* in Sanskrit) are essentially a program of fasting the mind. Gautama the Buddha himself realized, as did the ancient jnanis, the need for an environment suited to foster this fasting of the mind. As a result, people began to gather around the Buddha and live close to him. Once the historical Buddha passed away the spiritual path of Buddhism came into existence and is still to this day an efficient path to follow to end suffering and attain liberation.

The fasting the mind laboratories of Buddhism eventually led to the Zen tradition, which is almost identical to Advaita Vedanta in its teaching, philosophy, and spiritual science. Zen Buddhism is one of the most concise and mature paths to follow in the practice of fasting the mind. Its whole environment was originally set up in nature far away from worldly distractions. Joseph Campbell said of the Zen tradition, "You don't know where nature ends and art begins."[3]

The emphasis is on mindfulness in the same context as vipassana, which is why some believe Zen is the original teaching of Buddha because there is really no difference in essence between the two. Mindfulness in every moment is the core of both. This awareness training, mindfulness, naturally leads away from speaking much, since the focus is on the inner world. A Zen monastery offers us this time to fast the mind so that we can perceive *nirvana* in all life. Joseph Campbell explains the beauty of this nirvana experience in all life:

> *Nirvana* literally means "blown out"; the image is that once one has realized one's unity with what is called the Buddha mind—this is the Buddhist conception of *Brahman*—then one's individual ego is extinguished like a candle flame, and one becomes one with the great solar light.
>
> But when you get over there, you realize, I was here all the time. That's all, folks; we're there, and there is no place to go, and this is, basically, it. As Dr. Daisetz Suzuki, the Japanese Zen master, once said, "This world—with all its faults, all its crime, all its horror, all its banality, all its stupidity—is the golden lotus world." But you have to learn to see it in that dimension.[4]

This is the goal of Zen and all other spiritual-fasting clinics. The goal eventually is to leave the spiritual setting and perceive the nondual reality in all life, which gives spiritual oxygen to the whole world. This is the original characteristic of a *jivanmukta* or bodhisattva, meaning they have completely liberated themselves from separation and exist among society, not necessarily to teach us the way intentionally, but instead radiating this awareness into the world from simply *being* it. This return after fasting the mind is one reason why the *Chuang-tzu* text played a significant role in the formation of Chan Buddhism in China, which became Zen in Japan. Zen actually came into existence as a result of the marriage between the naturalist view of Taoism and Buddhist philosophy, thought to have happened when the great Buddhist master Bodhidharma, who is considered the traditional founder of Zen Buddhism, arrived in China from India. And it is the aspect of fasting the mind of both Taoism and Buddhism that made Zen a natural progression of Eastern thought and the beautiful path it is today.

The Taoist tradition itself had environments to facilitate the process of fasting the mind. This became the hermit tradition of China. If you wanted to know the nature of your existence, you would travel deep into the mountains to find a hermit master, a figure like Lao-tzu, for example. If you have that burning desire to "know thyself," you find a hermit master and they teach you the methods of fasting the mind, such as *nei gong* (internal martial arts that are a set of breathing, meditation, and spiritual practice disciplines associated with Taoism), which will dig deep into your subconscious content.

In exploring the spiritual clinics of the ancients, we come to Patanjali, the founding father of yoga. It is with Patanjali that a lot of the differing opinions of mind fasting coming from the Upanishadic era and early Buddhism begin to be synthesized. The original system of yoga is to fast the mind to realize our innate union with the source of the universe. With Patanjali, the science of mind fasting becomes more refined and clear to understand if the mental framework is solid for absorption.

As the science became more refined, more people had greater chances to apply it to their lives, bringing lasting peace not only to themselves but also contributing that peace to humanity. The spiritual clinics of the ancient masters gave rise to a method of scientific inquiry that is the framework for understanding the wheel of suffering—the wheel of samsara—and how to transcend it.

THE WHEEL OF SAMSARA FRAMEWORK

Samsara is a Sanskrit word that represents the wheel of suffering, or, more correctly, the wheel of time that makes us suffer through cycles of aimless drifting, wandering, or mundane existence. Samsara is what causes us to suffer day to day, year to year, and according to Indian tradition, life to life. The concept of samsara is that we are bound to time and suffer from its limitations. Keep in mind that the suffering referred to in the East is more about the mental sphere than the physical sphere. Physical suffering is inevitable—we are all going to get sick and die eventually. But it is our mental suffering that we endure the most through our lives. Mental suffering is based on the way we are conditioned to see the world from an isolated state of consciousness that develops the ego, which is a product of time.

Being bound to the limitations of time, we cannot perceive reality as it truly is, in the same way that a fish knows nothing about water. What is overshadowed by our samsaric perception of reality is *nirvana,* meaning extinction, freedom from suffering, and ultimately the unconditioned eternal reality that we experience as enlightenment. Our attachment to the idea of being a person with identity and problems, likes and dislikes, is what binds us to samsara, unable to recognize that nirvana is always present. This is the primary reason we suffer. We have invested too much time in defining ourselves as "somebody" in the vain hope that others will think we are special. But what makes each of us special is we have the opportunity to realize the nirvana world any time when we are ready to stop the charade of believing we are this permanent special identity. We are imprisoned by the cycle of samsara as a result. The problem for us is how to transcend the wheel of samsara to experience the splendor of the eternal nirvana.

To have this experience you need to realize that nirvana is ever present within you and not some heavenly abode you go to after physical death. It is foolish to think in this way because it is impossible for eternity to be in the future when it is beyond time and must only be *now*. This insight reveals that samsara and nirvana are not opposites, but are instead mutual and depend on each other. We cannot have the experience of eternity without the framework of time. It is right now where we experience eternity, but if we are not in this realm of time we cannot recognize it. This astounding paradox is expressed in the ancient auspicious symbol of the eternal knot or endless knot, known in Sanskrit as the *shrivatsa* (see figure 4.1), which is commonly found in Tibetan Buddhism.

The shrivatsa symbol gives an artistic representation of eternity and time in the world, nirvana and samsara. A consciousness dwelling in the nirvana world has escaped the wheel of suffering, the wheel of samsara. Enlightened individuals such as Gautama the Buddha experience

Figure 4.1. The shrivatsa symbol.

this consciousness because they have recognized that they suffer from believing they are this persona system built on time. The historical Buddha realized that our personality or ego is built on the parameters of time and is fundamentally impermanent, or *anicca* in Pali.

To transcend samsara is to transcend the notion of you. On the other hand, to be absorbed in nirvana is to realize that your real nature is eternal, but this can be known only when the sense of a person who suffers has been dropped, or, more important, fasted away. The great sages understood that what attracts us to time and not eternity is our psychic conditioning, which is built and reinforced by the process and experience of time and its changing panorama. This time construct in our heads is the wheel of samsara, where our latent suffering is born. The ancient science of fasting the mind is an antidote to heal these time-bound wounds so that we can eventually bask in the radiant beauty of eternity. To experience this nirvana state of consciousness we have to understand thoroughly the framework of suffering within the wheel of samsara before we explore the ancient framework of healing.

SAMSKARAS

Samskara in Sanskrit means "mental impressions or subliminal psychological imprints that are latent within our unconscious mind." We develop samskaras unknowingly from birth, and they drive our actions, interests, and desires until the day we die. It is also thought in India that some samskaras pass over from past lives if they haven't been cleansed from our psyche. Everything we experience in life, no matter whether we believe it is good or bad, are samskaras that we store in the subconscious. They remain dormant until activated by external stimuli if we don't learn how to work through them and release them.

Samskaras influence our reactions to the world. The bodily sensations we feel that drive our reactions toward fight or flight, craving or aversion, and identifying with pleasant or unpleasant circumstances are powered by our samskaras. Since they are the driving force behind such bodily reactions as fight or flight, samskaras give us the impression that they are very deep within the matrix of our nervous system. Our sensations, then, are powered by our samskaras. The conditioning we have experienced from birth is deep and can be alleviated only if we understand how to extinguish the fire of our samskaras that binds us to the cycle of samsara. William Hart explains in *The Art of Living: Vipassana Meditation* how our perception is plagued by the samskara (using the Pali *sankhara*) power base of the wheel of samsara:

> Every *sankhara* unleashes a chain of events that result in a new *sankhara*, which unleashes a fresh chain of events in an endless repetition, a vicious circle. Every time that we react, we reinforce the mental habit of reaction. Every time that we develop craving or aversion, we strengthen the tendency of the mind to continue generating them. Once the mental pattern is established, we are caught in it.
>
> For example, a man prevents someone from attaining a desired object. The thwarted person believes that man is very bad and dislikes him. The belief is based not on a consideration of the man's character, but only on the fact that he has frustrated the second person's desires. This belief is deeply impressed in the unconscious mind of the thwarted person. Every subsequent contact with that man is colored by it and gives rise to unpleasant sensation, which produces fresh aversion, which strengthens further the image. Even if the two meet after an interval of twenty years, the person who was thwarted long ago immediately thinks of that man as very bad and again feels dislike. The character of the first man may have changed totally in twenty years, but the second one judges him using the criterion of past experience. The reaction is not to the man himself, but to a belief about him based on the original blind reaction and therefore biased.[5]

The storehouse of samskaras confuses our perception of the world and oneself. Samskaras usually remain unconscious and as a result people incorrectly assume that the manifestation of their blind reactions is part of their character that cannot be changed. Our perception of good and bad is more often than not determined by our accumulated samskaras. This means we judge any new experience according to our samskaras rather than taking the experience for what it is in that moment. Our reactions in the present moment are essentially based on our past experiences.

It is difficult for anybody to act authentically in the here and now if their samskaras have not been alleviated. Many people who are interested in spirituality, especially from the East, believe they can just drop their samskaras with techniques such as self-inquiry or just trying to remain as the witness of everything going on in one's psychosomatic organism. Though both techniques are extremely valuable in revealing our samskaras through the awareness of our sensations, just having the awareness of them is not quite enough to alleviate them.

What we discover when we try such techniques just based on our conscious awareness of samskaras, whether we want to admit it or not, is that they persist and come out even stronger, which is evident in our body language and strong unconscious reactions. As a result our body language doesn't match up with our words.

For example, a person might claim she is content and joyful, but her facial expressions tell a completely different story. Because of this mental arm wrestling we tend to repress and suppress deeper aspects of ourselves. We discover these games that people play within their own mind when people intellectualize spiritual knowledge as absolutes. For example, many people practice self-inquiry, remaining in the "Who am I?" question in the hope of experiencing pure joy. As a result they use the inquiry to ignore their own latent samskaras coming up to the surface of the conscious mind so they suppress them even more. Their own samskaras then become more intense when they are activated and this is evident in their unconscious aggression and facial expressions, which they try to mask by intellectually stating that they are in a state of joy. As a result people play a subtle game of spiritual one-upmanship using words and phrases they heard from other sources to try and exhibit their worth over others. Disciples of a guru (or any spiritual teacher who takes on devotees) often exhibit this pathology as they believe they have transcended the ego, but instead only mimic the guru while their samskaras run wild unconsciously in their lives as they continue to dissociate from their emotions.

In trying to avoid our latent samskara power base under the illusion that it will just magically disappear, we dissociate the body from the mind, which leads to all sorts of psychological problems. When we pretend that we do not feel our physical sensations we sever our connection between the body and mind. To reintegrate the unity of the psychosomatic organism it is imperative to be conscious of our sensations so that we can better understand our samskaras. Those sensations arising out of the unconscious samskara field can be revealed if we examine how we blindly react to the world and perceive it. This is essential in making the unconscious conscious. The unconscious sensations of samskaras manifest through the habits and tendencies that come to life through our reactions.

Many of us react blindly to life from the habits and tendencies that we continually manifest in our experience unconsciously. These habits and tendencies are driven by our samskaras and they make up the second component of the wheel of samsara framework.

VASANAS

Vasanas are the habitual ways and latent tendencies that function on the unconscious level of mind. Vasanas are our habitual reactions to the sensations of samskaras within. Either good or bad, a vasana is a habit-forming tendency. Many habits are invariably toxic and linked to unconscious lazy tendencies when we have not begun the process of purging our samskaras. Because our samskaras are geared toward craving and aversion, and ultimately are self-interested, our vasanas will reflect their driving force. Thus, many people's vasanas bind them to suffering, as our habits are unhealthy and geared toward responding to stimuli rather than being aware of it.

Vasanas keep us locked in blind repetition where we begin to identify with our habits as who we are. To identify with our habits is absurd because we can change any time, but that is dependent on the self-work we engage in to expel our samskaras. If our vasanas are not revealed and exhausted, then our actions will always be plagued. The actions that are driven by our vasanas make up the third and last component of the wheel of samsara framework.

KARMA

In Sanskrit *karma* means "action." It comes from the Sanskrit root *kri*, which literally means "action." The New Age notion of karma as "cause and effect" is not correct but also not entirely false. Karma in its right definition consists of our actions and the results of our actions, meaning you don't act a certain way to get something in return, but instead action will always have a result no matter what the intention. People often say in referring to karma, "that is my karma," or "I have good karma," or "you have bad karma," and so on. These statements imply that there is a person who seeks to gain pleasurable benefits from life from their moral acts, or in the opposite spectrum one suffers unpleasant karma because of a lack of moral acts. This understanding of karma is absurd because it implies a system of reward and punishment, a system that the West has superimposed on karma due to the monarchical religions of the West. Thinking of karma in this way is egotistical because we are still self-interested and want something from God, as if God is a separate king of the world and we are his subjects. The concept of God as a king and the Western view of karma are absurd when contemplated deeply, and they have nothing in common with Eastern wisdom. (My book *Enlightenment Now* explores these contrasting views in more depth.)

The original and authentic understanding of karma in the East is that you just act naturally good without seeking any beneficial reward. There is only action in the present moment because in reality that is all there actually *is*. This natural way of acting truly good doesn't always mean it is always considered moral or ethical, as these are merely external standards of society, culture, and religion. Acting naturally good means to act spontaneously with what is needed in that moment—and every moment is different. What we believe are the effects of our karma are really only experienced in the present moment and not some future destination.

Our actions become impure when we want something in return, as if appeasing a kingly God who rewards and punishes. Having this view of karma is like children behaving well in the hopes of being rewarded by their parents—for example, with a nice bike for their birthday. The fact that adults continue in this way is all the proof we need that many adults never really reach adulthood. An ideal adult according to Eastern philosophy is someone who has complete responsibility for their actions in the present moment, without any thought of future results, because the future does not exist. Hence, the Eastern concepts of the universe and God are much more mature than the monarchical view of Western religions. Each action contains within it the seed of the future, but it is only the opposite view of the present because we can only experience either the past or future in the present moment. Our karma, then, can be pure only when we are empty of personality and seek no result because there is nobody there.

The sage's wisdom is to be free from karma, which means we don't stop acting but instead our actions are the result of having fasted the mind. Acting in this manner will begin to heal our samskaras because we are neither promoting those unconscious tendencies, nor are we accumulating more. But in many people's lives this awareness is not firmly established, and so we continue to act impurely because our actions are driven by our vasanas and powered by our samskaras. Our unconscious karmic actions result from our habits and tendencies, which are driven by our psychological impressions. Karma reinforces our samskaras, and our samskaras in turn fuel our karma. This vicious cycle is addressed by the classical yoga expounded by Patanjali, as Chip Hartranft explains:

> From Patanjali's perspective, any kind of volitional bodymind move-ment, whether mental or physical, constitutes a kind of action, or *karma*. Each action or volition leaves an impression (*samskara*) in the deepest part of memory, there to lie dormant for a time and then spring forth into some new, related action. This in turn will create fresh latent impressions, in a cycle of latency and activation.[6]

This is the vicious cycle of samsara. The actions with which we con-front the experience of life become the conditioning we unconsciously project into the world. Understanding this framework of samsara gives us the tools for transcending its vicious cycle.

THE SCIENCE OF HEALING THE WHEEL OF SAMSARA

To heal our actions (karma) and habits (vasanas) we have to fundamen-tally change ourselves. We need to eliminate the samskaras that bind us to this cycle. Yet we cannot just inwardly seek to change our samskaras because in many cases they manifest unconsciously through our actions. To fundamentally kill the roots of the samskara tree of suffering, we need to prune the branches back so far that the root system is starved of nourishment and consequently dies. It would be impossible to cut the samskara tree from the base and think that it will die that way because the roots will remain, that is, the samksaras will continue to function on the unconscious level. These roots are tenacious because they are deep subconscious impressions within our nervous system. So we prune the branches, beginning with karma and vasanas: we begin on the outer layer to change the inner layer.

We have to reverse the cycle from karma to samskaras in order to jump off the wheel of samsara. To dig into our samskaras we need to work backward, beginning with karma. When we realize the dilemma we are in, we start to examine our actions, questioning our habits and tendencies. This process is achieved through the science of mind fasting. Exploring our karmic actions, we need to start taking away the familiar distractions that alert us to act. We need to refrain from acting toward the world altogether for a certain amount of time. Developing a use for the scientific tools of fasting the mind is essential. The first tool we apply to our life is *viveka* (discrimination between the real and unreal in our mind), which I briefly mentioned earlier. To develop the ability of viveka we need to be able to reside in the nonsubjective witnessing state of pure awareness (Purusha) and be able to perceive the constant stream of mental movement and contents in your consciousness (prakrti) without identifying with it or reacting to it. In training to reside in pure awareness the use of viveka is like riding a bike, a vehicle to find our natural balance.

When we apply viveka to fundamentally change our actions it is coupled by another scientific tool of mind fasting: *vairagya,* which means "nonreaction" in Sanskrit. This means that we do not react to whatever we experience in the external world and within ourselves without first taking time to assimilate it. Only then can we choose if action is required. Chip Hartranft explains vairagya in his commentary of the *Yoga-Sutra of Patanjali* as "not getting stirred up" as we soften to experience. He states:

> The will to observe experience without reaction (*vairagya*) is the potential that brings about effortlessness. *Vairagya* literally means "not getting stirred up" and refers to the relationship that arises in the instant one perceives something. Most perceptions pluck the strings of our attachment to various likes, dislikes, or ideals. This sets off some type of mental or physical action, which may in turn create suffering. *Vairagya* is the willingness to let a phenomenon arise without reacting to it. In other words, one can allow any feature of consciousness—a thought, feeling, or sensation—to play

itself out in front of awareness without adding to its motion in any way. This subtracts more and more of the confusion from our experience, leading to profound stillness and clarity.

Thus *vairagya* reveals the newness and originality of the unfolding moment. As we let go of reacting in conditioned ways, we are jettisoning the learned patterns we have developed in the past to relate to every aspect of experience. To let go of these is to enter into a spontaneous and unpredictable present, unmodulated by wanting, aversion, or other forms of self-centeredness. Indeed, what gets "stirred up" in reaction always has to do with *me*. The sense of "I" is largely composed of reaction, being an encyclopedic anthology of likes and dislikes, and it infiltrates even our most altruistic thoughts and deeds.[7]

This ability of nonreaction is helped by developing viveka because we can become aware that our actions are driven by emotions, which cause us to act more like animals than humans.

When we look at the world and all the dramas that go on daily, much of it is caused by emotional people who react far too quickly to circumstances, and then as a result they regret their actions over time. For example, when there is a so-called terrorist attack, the media clumsily put their own spin on it, inciting hate among humanity against those perceived by the media as perpetrators. People then act irresponsibly and emotionally like animals, which is neither necessary nor intelligent. Just ask yourself: how many people have died in events related to 9/11 and the "War on Terror" from emotionally charged reactions and actions? We are talking at least over a million people and it didn't have to be that way if we understood viveka, vairagya, and ultimately that the boundaries that divide us are illusionary.

Vairagya fundamentally changes our unconscious reaction and begins to dig deep into our habit patterns. Applying vairagya to your life is a positive affirmation of trust that develops within the depths of your psyche. We begin to let life be as it will without our own personal agenda interfering with it. This is the wisdom of the great sage Lao-tzu and his awareness of the Tao, as the classic *Tao Te Ching* states:

> *In the pursuit of knowledge,*
> *every day something is added.*
> *In the practice of the Tao,*
> *every day something is dropped.*
> *Less and less do you need to force things,*
> *until finally you arrive at non-action.*
> *When nothing is done,*
> *nothing is left undone.*
>
> *True mastery can be gained*
> *by letting things go their own way.*
> *It can't be gained by interfering.*[8]

Because we develop viveka and employ vairagya we reveal our habitual actions that are normally unconscious and emotionally fueled. As a result we uncover our vasanas. Vairagya begins to change our vasanas because our actions are no longer driven by our habits and accustomed tendencies. In pruning our karmic actions we use viveka and vairagya to starve our vasanas of life. The more we can differentiate our habits from the eternal abode of pure awareness the less we react to them and make them manifest. Our vasanas are so deeply entrenched that most of us do not know we have these habitual patterns, and our reactions to the world can become predictable if they are analyzed for long enough. Functioning on the vasana level causes us to suffer if we don't apply vairagya and viveka to them. Nothing is fresh and spontaneous, but instead old and predictable. But if, on the other hand, we apply vairagya and viveka, they will begin to infiltrate the samskara matrix that has developed on the unconscious level. This is why the great Eastern sages say, "You need to burn out your vasanas if you want to know Brahman." Burning these vasanas out is done by fasting the mind with the scientific tools of viveka and vairagya, thereby cutting off the juice that fuels our karma and vasanas so that we can end their cyclical existence.

As a result we come down to the samskara level. Our samskaras begin to be fundamentally transformed when we have gone through the process of working through our karma and vasanas because these are the two limbs of samskaras. Having stopped our usual unconscious movement of actions and habits we arrive at the subtle sensory level, the root level of the samskaras. When we apply viveka and vairagya at this level we begin to observe the pure vibratory flux of sensations, known in Pali as *vedana*. In the ancient science of fasting the mind, we just observe these sensations objectively through viveka and vairagya. This is enhanced by the practice of anapanasati (awareness of respiration). Applying all three of these mind-fasting tools, we learn to observe vedana objectively for sustained periods. This objectivity of vedana has a profound effect on our samskaras.

When we fast the mind down to the sensory level we can avoid any new samskara reaction of craving or aversion, and thus we can begin to experience the ultimate reality within the unconscious. The unconscious here is more in the sense of what Carl Jung and Eastern philosophers call a "creative matrix of consciousness," as opposed to Sigmund Freud's negative view of a "holding tank of repressed materials." Once the samskaras have been cleaned out then the wisdom aspect of the unconscious begins to be felt and lived as the presence of Brahman or Tao in your consciousness. This experience of the ultimate reality dwelling deep within the unconscious is what leads to the complete liberation of mind, leading to a mind free from the development of attachment and from acquiring any new conditioning. This is the mind that has transcended the wheel of samsara and its components. This is the liberated mind of the great sages and mystics of antiquity. But it is not something that is isolated to a few great individuals who have come before us: it is available to any of us if we choose to fast the mind.

5
THE MODERN SCIENCE OF MIND FASTING

The modern research of cognitive science is nowadays exploring the ancient science of mind fasting. This may be indirectly linked to the ancient science of mind fasting, but nevertheless, cognitive science has come a long way to understanding the benefits of fasting the mind. Cognitive science has a lot of its own terminology, which we have to become familiar with so we can compare it to the ancient scientific framework we explored in the last chapter. Psychologists often like to make up their own terms, which separate them from the rest of the scientific community. In regard to cognitive science, the two main terms they use are *hot* and *cold*. Both of these refer to specific areas of the brain and their cognitive functions. Understanding them is significant in furthering our knowledge of mind fasting.

HOT COGNITION VERSUS COLD COGNITION

Hot cognition (known also as System 1) is the function of our mind and body that is automatic, spontaneous, fast, effortless, mostly unconscious, and thought to be emotionally driven. The hot system is found in the more primal part of the brain, which developed earlier in human evolution and which we associate with the unconscious. This system is what makes one's head turn unconsciously when a beautiful person passes by and drives us to eat that sweet even though it's unhealthy. The attraction to sweets is also linked to the way we evolved to seek sugar for momentary sustenance. The function of hot cognition is on the one hand divinely spontaneous, but on the other it can be a hindrance that leads us to eat unhealthy sweets, for example.

We bear witness to the spontaneous virtue of hot cognition in the miracles we discover in a sporting performance. It is what makes Johnathan Thurston of the NRL (Australia's National Rugby League) come up with the right play at the right time to get his team the North Queensland Cowboys over the try line consistently. And it is also what made Michael Jordan come up with the clutch play at the right time, like sinking a three-point shot to steal the game for his Chicago Bulls of the NBA (America's National Basketball Association). Spontaneously divine displays of sporting people, such as Thurston and Jordan, come into manifestation in a moment when there is no time to think about it: they act essentially from their gut instincts. And as we all know, when we have done something miraculous, if we are asked to do it again we begin to think about it, which thwarts our attempts to replicate it.

These spontaneous miracles we discover in other art forms, not just sport. Music, for example, is one art form where hot cognition brings the unconscious primal depths of the universe to life. The hot system allows musicians to play their instruments and feel the rhythm of the song without having to think about it: they are just present in that moment, devoid of a person thinking. And as is the case with sports, if you ask a musician to think while they play they would handicap their piece of music. In just being present and letting the unconscious hot cognitive system take over, or what the ancients called the unconscious wisdom of the body, we exhibit the spontaneous beauty of life devoid of categories. Musicians have an uncanny ability to be in this state, resulting from years of practice, which has influenced their hot system, even though many people are not conscious of this fact. We discover this ability in an improvisation among a group of musicians when they feel each other out and let spontaneity shine. Both of these examples of the beauty and magic of music and sports are the harmonious natural side of hot cognition. But, as I mentioned, the hot system can lead to evolutionary urges, such as seeking excessive amounts of sugar, that are unhealthy when the sugar we seek is refined and not natural. If such a desire goes untapped then we go down the path of obesity from sugar overconsumption. This untapped evolutionary aspect of hot cognition is offset by the part of the human brain that developed later in human evolution, which is where the cold cognitive function resides.

The cold cognition is found in the prefrontal cortex (PFC), which is the cerebral cortex that covers the front of the frontal lobe. It is believed that as we evolved we increasingly had to navigate through the world and all of its planetary obstacles for our survival as a species. This led to the evolution of the prefrontal cortex and, specifically, the dorsolateral prefrontal cortex and its executive functions, such as cognitive flexibility, inhibition, planning, working memory, and abstract reasoning. The prefrontal cortex is the house of the cold cognitive control functions. Cold cognition (known also as System 2) is the self-conscious, slow, deliberate, and effortful part of our mind, which we refer to as our self, the "I," in my case the "Jason," or who have you. It is the one who says no to the sugar sweet. Yet this is not to say that the hot system is not concerned about your health and well-being. On the contrary, it adapted to the requirements of evolution that are more ancient than the convenient circumstances of the modern day. Edward Slingerland explains this dilemma of cold and hot cognition in regard to our evolution, health, and well-being:

> So if I say that I had to force myself not to reach for that second helping of tiramisu, there is a more than metaphorical struggle going on. My conscious, cold system, which is concerned about long-range

issues like health and weight gain, is fighting to control the more instinctive hot system, which really likes tiramisu and doesn't share my cold system's concerns about the consequences. This isn't because hot cognition doesn't take future consequences into account. The problem is that this system's conception of relevant consequences was fixed a long time ago, evolutionarily speaking, and is fairly rigid. "Sugar and fat: *good*" was for most of our evolutionary history a great principle to live by, since acquiring adequate nutrition was a constant challenge. For those of us fortunate enough to live in the industrialized world, however, sugar and fat are so widely and freely available that they no longer represent unqualified goods—on the contrary, allowing ourselves to indulge in them to excess has a variety of negative consequences. The great advantage of cold cognition is that it is capable of changing its priorities in light of new information.[1]

Though cold cognition may help us with our dietary choices, it can be physiologically expensive if it is overemployed. We tend to have this energy depletion when we have overexerted our will to achieve something. When our conscious mind (cold cognition) exerts a lot of effort we feel as though we have run a marathon. Problems with the cold cognition begin to happen when we essentially try too hard to achieve whatever end that may be. We try too hard in accordance with our social and cultural conditioning. Employing our cold cognition to accord with the sense of good or bad, pleasant or unpleasant, and sense activity, leads one into self-interest. The overuse of the cold cognitive controls leads to radical individualism and people becoming egocentric. This cold self-centeredness is what causes many problems we have in the world, both individually and collectively.

In overcompensating for the cold cognition we develop this sense of being a person separate from the environment. As I've mentioned before, the ancient Eastern science of mind fasting holds that when you think you are an individual it leads not only to your own suffering but also the suffering of the world. Yet humanity is progressively moving down this individualistic path, which is why self-interest and materialism are the central focus in the modern world. As individuals we seek to stand out above the crowd, as if this illustrates success. But this charade of trying to be better than other people according to the illusion of being a person is exhausting and inevitably doesn't last. This tendency to overcompensate for the cold over the hot is culturally connected to how human civilization evolved on this planet.

THE EVOLUTION OF HUMAN COGNITION

As the human species began to move to different locations on the planet, our minds naturally adapted to the environments and circumstances that we confronted. This is highly significant in regard to which parts of the brain were in function and the worldview that was shaped accordingly. This is evident when we explore Asiatic and Western cultures from before the Common Era. When we go back to the first two millennia BCE some of the biggest civilizations were the Greek and Chinese cultures. Due to environmental factors, both civilizations developed cognitively different.

When we explore the evolution of ancient Greece we discover mainly small groups of people spread out along a vast area of the Mediterranean coastline. Living in smaller communities meant that the sustenance for survival was oriented toward more individualistic activities. Hunting, herding, and fishing were the main sources of food and labor that the Greeks were engaged in, and they are very individualistic activities. Contrary to the Greeks, the ancient Chinese civilization evolved around the Yellow River valley of northern China. The ancient Chinese lived in larger communities due to the need for establishing large irrigation systems for rice cultivation. Rice cultivation requires a lot of people and is a collective activity, as we still see today in Asia. American psychologist Richard E. Nisbett explains this in his book *The Geography of Thought:*

> The ecology of China, consisting as it does primarily of relatively fertile plains, low mountains, and navigable rivers, favored agriculture

and made centralized control of society relatively easy. Agricultural peoples need to get along with one another—not necessarily to like one another (think of the stereotype of the crusty New England farmer)—but to live together in a reasonably harmonious fashion. This is particularly true for rice farming, characteristic of southern China and Japan, which requires people to cultivate the land in concert with one another. But it is also important wherever irrigation is required, as in the Yellow River Valley of north China, where the Shang dynasty (from the eighteenth to the eleventh century B.C.) and the Chou dynasty (from the eleventh century B.C. to 256 B.C.) were based. In addition to getting along with one's neighbors, irrigation systems require centralized control and ancient China, like all other ancient agricultural societies, was ruled by despots. Peasants had to get along with their neighbors and were ruled by village elders and a regional magistrate who was the representative of the king (and after the unification of China, of the emperor). The ordinary Chinese therefore lived in a complicated world of social constraints.

The ecology of Greece, on the other hand, consisting as it does mostly of mountains descending to the sea, favored hunting, herding, fishing, and trade (and—let's be frank—piracy). These are occupations that require relatively little cooperation with others. In fact, with the exception of trade, these economic activities do not strictly require living in the same stable community with other people. Settled agriculture came to Greece almost two thousand years later than to China, and it quickly became commercial, as opposed to merely subsistence, in many areas. The soil and climate of Greece were congenial to wine and olive oil production and, by the sixth century B.C., many farmers were more nearly businessmen than peasants. The Greeks were therefore able to act on their own to a greater extent than were the Chinese. Not feeling it necessary to maintain harmony with their fellows at any cost, the Greeks were in the habit of arguing with one another in the marketplace and debating one another in the political assembly.[2]

The environmental factors that both cultures encountered deter-mined which part of the brain developed further. In ancient Greece life was oriented more toward individualism as a result of the environment. This individualistic perspective exercises more of the cold cognitive con-trols in the prefrontal cortex. As a result people began to be increas-ingly analytical, not because the people were naturally like that, but because that was what was required to sustain life due to the environ-ment. This tendency toward the function of the cold cognitive controls was the seed of the Western psychological trait of analysis. The Western analytical perspective has become the primary cognitive response to life around the world. Beginning in the West, as a result of analyti-cal thinking, everything is dissected, unpacked, and pulled apart in the hope of always coming to a logical conclusion. Yet we are blind to the fact that our logical conclusions are based on our conditioning, which is subjective and not objective.

This analytical view has influenced the modern world tremen-dously, starting in ancient Greece. The Western view of the universe, God, society, and culture is almost always analytical. The analytical view gave birth to linear thinking, which corrupted Western institu-tions. For example, Western religions take on a very linear and authori-tarian view of God as an egotistical ruler, which results in a political view of the universe, rather than a more natural view. The idea that God created this world and we are subject to him as a king comes from the analytical view of how individuals apply themselves to life. This means we think of a universe that is created, in the same sense of how we build a home: from the outside as an external agent. Western reli-gions think of God in this way, and it has influenced most Western religions deeply. For example, Jesus was the son of a carpenter and also the son of God, and both are seen as builders.

The cold analytic view is attracted to what stands out rather than the relationships of the background to the foreground. Western thought tends to dissect and categorize anything—God, for example—making it the pinnacle of thought, without realizing that if you highlight one object you exclude the rest, which ultimately implies duality rather than the oneness of God. Because of analytical thinking those in the West divide the world into opposites that are separate and isolated. God and humanity are opposites, likewise black and white, female and male, and so on. This way of thinking is completely opposite to that of the East and many indigenous cultures.

There is psychological evidence to prove this difference. Research shows that when Westerners and Easterners are shown the same images they each describe different features and focus on different aspects. For example, one of the better-known research tools is a picture that shows a large object in the foreground and a background composed of smaller objects. One such image shows a big fish in the front while the background is composed of much smaller fish and coral (see figure 5.1).

Looking at this image in the research laboratory, a group of Westerners and Easterners were asked what they see. The majority of

Figure 5.1. The differences between foreground and background.
By Dao Stew.

the Westerners described the big fish in the foreground, showing little or no awareness of the background. The majority of the Easterners, on the other hand, described the background and its relation to the foreground. This same test has been done many times with similar results. The conclusion of such research illustrates that Westerners are cognitively conditioned to perceive things that stand out due to analytical thinking, which results in a tendency to divide life into categories and objects. The Easterners, on the other hand, are cognitively oriented toward perceiving the world holistically, likely resulting from the collective tendency to perceive life through context and relationships. Both of these different perceptions of life gave birth to the social, cultural, and spiritual philosophies that Easterners and Westerners tend to unconsciously uphold. As Richard E. Nisbett states:

> So long as economic forces operate to maintain different social structures, different social practices and child training will result in people focusing on different things in the environment. Focusing on different things will produce different understandings about the nature of the world. Different worldviews will in turn reinforce differential attention and social practices. The different worldviews will also prompt differences in perception and reasoning processes—which will tend to reinforce worldviews.[3]

Focusing on relationships and context is a hallmark of Eastern thought. This Eastern view naturally came about because of the environmental factors, which were mainly community driven in the East. For example, in ancient China what was good for me on a personal level was not necessarily good for the community. And because the main source of food was rice, it was not beneficial for everyone to pursue personal interests. Social harmony was imperative in those times, over and above egocentric desires. As a result the cold cognitive functions were not overly employed because the naturalness of the hot system took over the individual, and so the community could work in unison.

Over time this hot cognitive approach to life led to the holistic perception of the world. The holistic view comes from always considering what is best for the greater whole at the expense of your own interests. The holistic view is a state of consciousness that is always mindful of the big picture, while the analytical view keeps us blind to the big picture because it is lost in the detail of one's own mind and circumstances that are driven by our personal agenda.

The philosophies and spiritual traditions that result from the more holistic Eastern perception of life, such as Hinduism, Buddhism, Taoism, and Confucianism, tend to reflect the view of the totality and how important it is to act in accord with the greater perspective, be that Brahman/Tao, society, or what have you. The wisdom traditions are then based on mutuality and a sense of mystery rather than thinking we know everything. One idea prevalent in the Eastern wisdom traditions is that opposites are mutual, and in their deepest essence one and the same. For example, God dwells in humanity. Also, there is no beginning of night and day, as they are one process. The Chinese concepts of yin (feminine, receptive, earth, cooling energy) and yang (masculine, active, heaven, hot energy) are only apparent opposites when we compensate for one over the other, but when they are in balance we discover their intrinsic unity. Even when we start out in the womb we are all the same. We can't see this obvious reality when we are overly dependent on the analytical cold cognition. To overuse the cold analytical cognition will exhaust you physiologically, causing the hot system to take over to compensate, taking the "I," the sense of self, out of the equation. As we become exhausted, we loosen our grip on the daily dramas of life and lose our apparent control so that the unconscious wisdom of the universe can take over. In losing control you gain the kind of control you were always after, which is divinely powerful. This is the wisdom of the East.

That power arises from the unconscious regions of the brain, which are the regions of the brain that were primarily in use in ancient China that results from the collectivist environmental factors. Not many sages, philosophers, and deep thinkers, except for political leaders and royalty, were self-interested in the ancient East because that led to selfishness and the illusion of a personal identity. In both ancient times and today the problems and suffering in the world come from the same place: the wrong perception of an "I" separate from the universe. The idea of the person that you think you are eclipses your understanding that you are one with the universe as the universe. Our mind is plagued with contents that we identify with, without sensing the pure awareness deep within that we truly are.

When we think of "I" we are only thinking of the cold cognition, the troubleshooter that scans the environment for obstacles based on our conditioning, what Chuang-tzu would call the human flaw of qing (*qing* means "species-specific essence," and in relation to humans it means the "ability to discern between this and that," which Chuang-tzu believes is a fundamental flaw). Since our fundamental problem in ancient times is the same as today, both ancient and modern sciences can be combined in understanding the framework to eventually downregulate the sense of "I."*

COGNITIVE SCIENCE IN THE WHEEL OF SAMSARA

Cognitive science can be applied to the wheel of samsara, and actually contributes to its understanding. Combining both ancient and modern sciences of mind fasting, we need to fit the concepts of hot and cold cognition to samskaras, vasanas, and karma. Merging cognitive science and ancient Eastern sciences makes it easier to assimilate it and to apply it to our lives.

When we explore how our samskaras become hardwired, we need to break it down from the top down, as I mentioned in the last chapter.

Downregulate is used here as a term referring to decreasing or lowering the strong sense of "I" ego you have within your mind, the cold cognitive function within the prefrontal cortex.

But in this case we are taking a different view. As each of us are brought into this "world of ignorance," as Manly P. Hall stated, our cold cognition is taught to apply itself to the accepted indoctrination of society, culture, and religion. Our accepted education is a good example of this ignorance. As soon as we start going to school we are taught whatever the society believes is acceptable. During this arduous process of indoctrination our cold cognition is overused to the point of permanent psychological damage.

Evidence of this is found in South Korea, where teen suicide rates are one of the highest in the world. These suicides are the result of an education system in South Korea that demands teens go to school and study for sometimes sixteen hours a day. Psychological damage is inevitable if our cold cognition has to be engaged for sixteen hours a day. There is no time for adequate rest and for the hot processes of the mind to function naturally. This is why when you are on the subway early in the morning in Seoul you find students completely knocked out from mental exhaustion, where not even a comet crashing into the Earth could wake them up. I know this because I witnessed this exhaustion firsthand while living in Seoul. Yet I'm only using South Korea as an extreme example.

The system that is built around us in any part of the world, except for indigenous cultures, is focused on overexercising cold cognition. This has been done for good reason from the established order's point of view. The system, no matter whether it is government, royalty, education, religion, corporate, or any component of society, and culture, is oriented toward hijacking the cold cognition, stealing our attention, in the hope that eventually the system will become part of our samskaras that drive us unconsciously through life. Deliberately or not, the system is clever enough to have stolen our attention and fundamental awareness of ourselves. As a result, the way our world is structured is that our cold cognition is overemployed to influence and eventually become our personal traits that are our samskaras.

We are trained from birth the accepted social, cultural, and religious indoctrination so that we not only believe what we are told but that we actually become it in the sense that we think these concepts are who we are. In overtraining cold cognition it slowly becomes our hot cognitive reactions to the world. Hot cognition is the new simplistic view of samskaras, vasanas, and karma. As our cold cognition is trained so will this training become our hot cognition. This is not always all bad in terms of indoctrination.

For example, you may undergo years of music training, which will eventually become part of your hot cognition, what is commonly known as muscle memory. After years of practice you can just pick up the violin—if that is your instrument—and let the magic of Bach vibrate from it to enlighten the ears of others. You don't have to think about it in order to play this piece of Bach, because it is part of your hot cognition, your samskara makeup. This is a virtuous hot state that you bring into the world because art itself has no agenda—this is why it is beautiful and divine. We don't have to think about its beauty because we know what we hear without thoughts interfering.

But in general this is not the case. In general we are trained a certain way to uphold a certain system, which invariably does not truly benefit or serve us. This is done by providing a method and system for our cold cognition to follow in the hope of turning that into hot cognitive reactions. Eventually these hot cognitive reactions become the unconscious fuel, which becomes the basis of the war we are waging against our own mind, as I briefly mentioned in the introduction. The psychological indoctrination is so deep that if it continues to live in us unexamined by a sufficient method such as mind fasting, then we will continue to suffer and not know why.

When our cold cognition has been put through the rigors of indoctrination and repetition it becomes our hot samskaras. And then we exhibit two other hot components that we know from our ancient science of mind fasting: vasanas and karma. The irony and revelation of unifying the ancient and modern science of mind fasting is that when we manifest our hot karma on the wheel of samsara it is our cold cognition that has to deal with the consequences of our hot samskaras, and this ultimately produces more karma if the pattern is not revealed. It is a never-ending wheel until we become aware of this process. We—and no one else—suffer at the hands of ourselves psychologically. Our cold cognition is constantly dealing with our hot samskaras, vasanas, and karma that were implemented by our cold cognition in the first place. The person you actually think of as yourself, with all of your beliefs, desires, and attachments, is only your cold cognition in conflict with the unconscious and untamed hot cognitive processes. It becomes a battle between the ruler mind (cold cognition) that you identify with and the hot cognitive processes of the body that we believe are untamed, animalistic, and ultimately unconscious. This battle is Plato's charioteer analogy, which is similar to the Chinese water manager metaphor, as Edward Slingerland explains:

> This metaphor of mind as master of an otherwise unruly body is a common one. Plato's mind, for instance, is a charioteer, trying to control a team of wild horses that represent hot cognition in various guises. In China, a more common metaphor has been water control: an irrigation manager trying to channel water to where it is needed, or divert it in order to avoid flooding. This makes a great deal of sense for a culture completely at the mercy of the powerful, and erratic, Yellow River, which was a source of water and fertility for the entire Yellow River Valley but was prone to jumping its banks and causing widespread devastation. In all of these folk and religious models, "we" (the charioteer, water manager) need to exert force to control the hot power of nature (animals, water). Although this dichotomy between a rational person and irrational force captures our internal experience of self-control, it's important to keep in mind that it isn't really accurate from a scientific perspective. Self-control is *all* about the embodied mind, in that certain regions of the brain strengthen some neural pathways at the expense of others. We identify with the cognitive control regions, and personify

them as rational agents, only because they also happen to be the seat of consciousness and language—they are the part of our brain that writes the script of our lives and takes all the credit.[4]

But according to the prevailing ancient wisdom of the East we would be wrong to assume that our hot cognition/samskaras is naturally untamed and animalistic. As I've mentioned, our training of cold cognition warps our nature, and thereby inevitably becomes our hot cognition. To assume that our nature (hot cognition) is fundamentally flawed, we would have to side with Confucius in the belief that we are mere beasts until we have had proper training. The proper training according to Confucius is his own philosophy, which definitely is enough to suspect something is up as no one philosophy is the be all and end all. Yet if we are to take the view of some of the more influential sages of ancient times we must conclude that it is our overuse of the cold cognition that is the problem. We know Chaung-tzu supports this view, with his description of qing and fasting the mind. He emphasizes the need to fast the cold cognition away so our spiritual desires, our natural and spontaneous hot cognition, can take over and bring us into accord with the Tao.

This view that we are naturally good until we are tampered with by the world is supported by Lao-tzu, Gautama the Buddha, Mencius, Patanjali, and Shankara. We have warped our nature from training and identifying only with cold cognition. Naturally we had none of these flaws originally, but instead they were conditioned into us. Confucius may argue with that and say that sexual urges rise naturally and can cause a lot of harm if acted upon carelessly. But the point he is missing is that these actions are careless only when we lose our natural function of pure awareness to observe our sensations, rather than letting our emotions that are built on our cold cognitive processes to take over. Acting carelessly and without awareness leads us to not feel sympathy or love for another, as we seek to gain whatever from the situation fueled by our attraction to pleasure. Essentially our rational mind (cold cognition) gets in the way of nature because it is seeking to fulfill the desires of self-interest.

THE NATURE OF OX MOUNTAIN IS GOOD

Mencius, a great Chinese sage of the Warring States period, believed that human nature was fundamentally good. He had some profound ways to explain this innate goodness. One analogy he uses is the child near the well. The child is at the well retrieving water for their family and the child is about to fall in because of the weight of the bucket. If you were to witness this, what would your initial reaction be? Most people would say that they would do anything humanly possible to save the child from falling in. This is natural and comes from a place deeper than the cold cognitive processes of thoughts and rationality. You just have a natural feeling beneath the cold cognition, and this is our natural hot cognitive state. In that moment there is no time for deliberation—you just act spontaneously and that action is naturally virtuous, good, pure, and selfless.

It could only be otherwise if we were under the hypnosis of being a separate entity to the child. Amazingly we are so overtrained and indoctrinated that in some cases the cold rational mind stops us from helping that child due to our selfish self-interests. Essentially, our cold cognition, which we identify with and believe is who we are, would scan the environment and sense danger for ourselves so we would suppress our natural impulse to help another. This is the birth of the "innocent bystander." Naturally we are good but we have become toxified from the environment we have been raised in.

Mencius tackles this problem with an analogy called "Ox Mountain":

> The woods on Ox Mountain were once beautiful! On account of its being on the edge of a large country, it had been attacked with axes and hatchets, and then how could it remain beautiful? The refresh-

ing breezes of day and night, and the moisture provided by rain and fog, did not fail to give rise to sprouts of vegetation. But cows and sheep have been repeatedly pastured there, and for that reason it has remained desolate. People observe its denuded state and assume that it never had any good resources. But how could this state be the true nature of this mountain?[5]

Like the mountain, human nature has growing in it four different kinds of sprouts: empathy, righteous indignation, ritual propriety, and wisdom. But these sprouts are constantly being consumed, so that people may outwardly seem depleted of these good qualities. It wasn't Ox Mountain's nature that was flawed; it was the environment it was in that gave it toxicity. Similarly, our environment warps our nature through the process of cold cognitive training according to the toxic principles of the society. We become the society as a result of our hot cognition being conditioned to act and think a certain way. The problem, then, is we identify with the cold cognition and navigate through reality with it according to the hot cognition/samksaras that have been implemented by its training. So the question, then, is How do we get out of this bind of building the illusion of a person around only the cold cognition?

6

DOWNREGULATING THE SENSE OF "I" WITH MIND FASTING

When we overcompensate for the cold cognitive functions we begin to make distinctions between our mind and body as if they are separate. As in Plato's charioteer analogy, he believed our body is an untamed beast that the ruler mind needs to gain control of. But as we've discussed, this is not entirely true. Our body can act beastlike but that occurs due to the cold cognitive training that we implement deep in our hot cognition creating samskaras, vasanas, and ultimately karma.

There is a wisdom consciousness of the body that dwells deep within the archaic unconscious and comes to life when the sense of the cold cognitive ruler has been moved out of the way. What keeps many of us locked away from this divine beauty and creative spontaneity is that we have bought into the illusion that this cold cognition is "us" and that the hot cognition is something separate and isolated from who we are, almost as if the bodily hot cognition is a hindrance that disturbs our mental life. This mind-body dualism is accepted by many people in the world, either consciously or unconsciously. We refer to *my body* as if it is a vehicle we are locked in against our will.

If we observe our psychosomatic organism closely, we will see that our mind and body cannot be separate, as they are a bundle of nerves and organs that work harmoniously in unison. Our nervous system is not compartmentalized; it is one system. In a lot of traditions of the East, the mind is thought of as the whole body due to the intelligence and electromagnetic current of the nervous system. For example, to be blatantly obvious, when we stretch and go for a run our mind enters a state of clarity and equanimity. So if the body and mind are separate and distinct, then physical exercise would have no effect in the mind. We know this is true but do not consider it.

In the ancient East they were attentive to the propensity to think the body and mind were separate, and so they sought to design systems for people to realize their innate nonduality. Hatha yoga and t'ai chi, for example, came into existence for people to realize there is no separation between mind and body. Essentially, they were designed to get you out of the head and into the whole body, all the way down to the subtle level where you become conscious of the vital force within your being, known as *prana* in Sanskrit and *qi* in Chinese.

Identifying too much with the "I," or cold cognition, has always been a problem. In the ancient East, though, they didn't seek to eliminate cold cognition entirely. On the contrary, they realized that cold cognition is one of two primary functions of the mind—the other being hot cognition—even though they did not use these terms. They understood that the problem resides in the overuse of cold cognition leading our mind to think in terms of duality, which in turn begins the process of believing you are this person opposed by the rest of the universe. When we do this, we block our consciousness from allowing the wisdom of the universe to express itself through us, because the sense of "I" has blocked the stream, that is, the Tao. The ancient Eastern masters understood there is no "you" as a person separate from the body. To them mind is body and body is mind.

There is one different dimension from this, as I've mentioned, which is Purusha, Atman, and Brahman, that is only evoked and experienced when we have an integration of hot and cold cognition that facilitates a state of undifferentiated consciousness. This is known as the embodied mind, where both cold and hot cognition are integrated. We realize that they are not separate parts of the mind-body but just different functions that have developed for us to experience this universe in its entire splendor. This experience of the embodied mind is what is known in Chinese as *wu-wei*, which means "effortless action," "nondoing," and ultimately a "psychological state of no force." It is a state of consciousness at complete ease and moves gracefully and efficiently. The state of wu-wei could be best explained as intelligent spontaneity.

The embodied mind is a higher state of consciousness that experiences life with the totality of being rather than being centered in either body/hot cognition or mind/cold cognition. Living from the embodied mind state reduces the cold cognition from a stiff person who opposes the world to its natural function, which is purely a way to interface with the world without allowing those experiences to cling to one's being creating samskaras. Essentially, you become egoless without losing your sense of self from the embodied mind. It is like the ancient Zen parable:

> *Before enlightenment*
> *chopping wood*
> *carrying water.*
> *After enlightenment*
> *chopping wood*
> *Carrying water.*[1]

The sense of a person, or "I," begins to lose its power within your consciousness. You become free to experience life purely with no agenda. This is the beginning of the spiritual process of yoga, the reunification of you with the Divine, the realization that Atman is Brahman. The sense of you, the person, the ego, becomes absorbed in Brahman. Your whole life changes to the tune of the universal drum, *om* (representative of the primordial vibration/sound). You become free from the mental prison you've built for yourself. Cold cognition loses its dictatorship over hot cognition and nature begins to finally blossom through you as your fundamental nature, li. The problem for us is how to achieve this while we are still functioning predominately with the cold cognitive regions of the brain. In the ancient East they obviously encountered this dilemma as well. Their focus was therefore on how to downregulate the sense of "I," the cold cognition.

DOWNREGULATING COLD COGNITION

There are numerous methods for downregulating our cold cognition. Some are obvious, and some aren't. A lot of us know these methods because we explore them in our lives at particular moments. Exercise is one method that many of us are unaware of. When we exercise, especially cardiovascular exercise, we get that sense of effortlessness (wu-wei) because the sense of a person disappears due to the automatic functions of the body. As a result, the unconscious wisdom of the mind-body has downregulated the prefrontal cortex. Neuroscientist Arne Dietrich has researched the effects of what exercise does to our cognitive abilities. He has coined the term *transient hypofrontality* in regard to the downregulation of the cold cognitive control regions of the prefrontal cortex that occurs during physical exercise. Intense physical exercise puts a lot of stress on the body and so the parts of the body that are not essential begin to shut down. Our prefrontal cortex is one of those regions that becomes disengaged. Our state of consciousness during intense exercise lacks the sense of "I" that is present with cold cognition. As Arne Dietrich explains:

> Some of the phenomenologically unique features of this state such as experiences of timelessness, living in the here and now, reduced awareness of one's surroundings, peacefulness (being less analytical),

and floating (diminished working memory and attentional capacities), are consistent with a state of frontal hypofunction. Even abstruse feelings such as the unity with the self and/or nature might be more explicable, considering that the prefrontal cortex is the very structure that provides us with the ability to segregate, differentiate, and analyze the environment.[2]

Though this is the case with exercise, it is a cognitive state that can be achieved only temporarily because you cannot exercise *all* the time. In fact, if you don't exercise in moderation then you may face complete burnout. So using exercise as a method to tap into this sense of selflessness is only temporary and not linked to fasting the mind permanently. This feeling of relaxation from physical exercise is similar to what we get from sex. Sex is another method of downregulating the "I," where we engage in an act of intimacy with another person. During the sexual act we show parts of ourselves psychologically that are hardly ever revealed at other times. The sense of you as a person during a consensual sexual act is downregulated, as you absorb your entire being in that interconnected moment. Yet, as with exercise, if sex is not in moderation then it can lead to all sorts of problems. And the fact is we can't have sex all the time either, so this is only a temporary method of downregulating your "I." Other more popular methods are also linked to pleasure.

Psychedelics, like ayahuasca and psilocybin, completely downregulate the prefrontal cortex and put you into a spiritual dimension that dwells within the unconscious hot cognitive regions of the mind. And yet, we cannot have psychedelics all the time without doing physical and psychological damage. Another popular method, which is also a psychoactive, is marijuana. Marijuana is an extremely popular method because it downregulates the cold cognition with a chilled-out effect. But as we know with marijuana, it can lead to excessive laziness and also damage our cognition if it is not taken in moderation. (However, the damage done by marijuana and other psychedelics is small in comparison with that of the world's preferred choice of downregulating cold cognition: alcohol.)

Alcohol is the accepted drug that many people use to escape their life's dramas and just enjoy themselves, temporarily avoiding inevitable pain. We enjoy alcohol because it naturally downregulates our cold cognition so we can then communicate and experience the world authentically with no agenda. That is up until a certain point. As we all know too well, if not taken in moderation alcohol is not only bad for your health but also can lead to becoming completely switched off, so that your actions become more animal than human. If we drink in moderation we can sometimes release genuineness in ourselves, which our cold cognition held prisoner. As a result alcohol is the preferred beverage of choice and consumed at parties and social gatherings to help break the ice, get people out of their shell, let go, and have a good time together. That is, alcohol can be an effective "social lubricant." You witness this when two people have a few drinks and they express their true feelings for each other by telling them that they love each other or in other cases when people deal tenderly with latent issues they have had with each other. Our unconscious attraction to intoxicants is about letting go of the cognitive control regions so the "real you" can be free. As Edward Slingerland states:

> Alcohol, kava, cannabis, magic mushrooms, you name it: any intoxicant that people can get their hands on quickly comes to play a central role in social occasions, both formal and informal. In ancient China, no major treaty was signed without first bringing everyone together in an extended, alcohol-soaked banquet. In fact, this is one feature of Chinese culture that has not changed a bit in over four thousand years. Any modern businessperson hoping to ink a deal with Chinese partners had better get his or her liver in shape first.
>
> On a less formal level, this is no doubt why intoxicants are a universal feature of all sorts of human social gatherings, from casual cocktail parties to fraternity mixers. Not only is getting drunk pleasant, it also typically causes people to get along more freely and easily (at least to a certain point, after which the drunken fights break

out). Intoxication enhances cooperation in at least two ways. First of all, it reduces social faking by inhibiting cognitive control centers. Second, if we all get drunk together, we create a situation of mutual vulnerability that makes trust easier to establish. Getting drunk is essentially an act of mental disarmament. In the same way that shaking right hands with someone assures them that you're not holding a weapon, downing a few tequila shots is like checking your prefrontal cortex at the door. See? No cognitive control. You can trust me.[3]

The Eastern sage recognized that methods such as I've mentioned are not sufficient because they only have a temporary effect. I do not condone or support any of these methods that I have mentioned thus far. Realizing this, the Eastern sage turned their attention inward to explore the depths of consciousness for answers. Those adventurers of consciousness came back with the meditative techniques that we still use today. These meditative practices are a natural therapy for downregulating the cold cognitive controls. They are the medicine that is needed for a prolonged state of wu-wei. These practices include not only the fasting-the-mind practice of vipassana, but also a similar method focused not on the senses but instead on nothingness.

THE MEDITATIVE EYE OF SPIRIT

A meditative practice in the East was developed to starve the cold cognitive controls. This practice is technically known as open awareness meditation. This is an objectless meditation that we engage with a simple, stable posture while we try to observe the mind in the hope of silencing and emptying it through focusing on our breath or by fixing our attention on something in the environment. This type of meditation, like vipassana, has a positive effect on mental concentration, reaction time, motor skills, and sensory sensitivity to the environment. The more we practice open awareness meditation, the less we need anchors for our awareness, such as focusing on breath or something in the environment. Our consciousness becomes naturally spacelike, not in the sense of blank empty space, but instead just like the space that contains the whole universe. It is an ever-present empty state, but not averse to an experience coming into it. The only difference between this spacelike consciousness and the usual full mind-cup consciousness is that when an experience comes into the former it is not held on to, eventually becoming our samskaras. Instead, the experience essentially leaves no samskara footprints in the mind because the mind is no longer "sticky." This is the cognitive function of the enlightened mind, the Zen mind.

The practice of open awareness meditation and the result of an enlightened consciousness that comes from it, was wisdom brought with Bodhidharma from India to China where it mixed with Chinese Taoism and finally became Chan Buddhism in China, which eventually migrated to Japan and became Zen Buddhism. In the same fashion as vipassana, Zen, *Chan* in Chinese, or *Dhyana* in Sanskrit, is a method of meditation we apply to our everyday life that begins to downregulate the sense of "I." As a result, we begin to see reality as it truly is without dissecting it into apparent duality. Naturally we begin to perceive reality from the hot holistic cognition. In China this was thought of as "seeing with spirit." This is evident in the Cook Ting story in the *Chuang-tzu*. Cook Ting explains to Lord Wen-hui how he cuts up oxen so effortlessly:

> What I care about is the Way, which goes beyond skill. When I first began cutting up oxen, all I could see was the ox itself. After three years I no longer saw the whole ox. And now—now I go at it by spirit and don't look with my eyes. Perception and understanding have come to a stop and spirit moves where it wants. I go along with the natural makeup, strike the big hollows, guide the knife through the big openings, and follow things as they are. So I never touch the smallest ligament or tendon, much less a main joint.[4]

He encounters the ox with his spirit, and this allows the spiritual energy of the Tao to take over. Seeing from spirit and being in psychological effortlessness (wu-wei) is the same state of consciousness as the inner discrimination of viveka. Viveka is a natural awareness arising from open awareness meditation. Open awareness meditation facilitates seeing from spirit, viveka. Yet we must not make the mistake of thinking that the discrimination of viveka is the same as the subjective discrimination of the cold cognitive regions of the brain. Viveka is different from cold cognition because it is not subjective. Cold cognition is always there to some extent, but the difference is that viveka is a pure awareness of the hot unconscious regions of the brain when the prefrontal cortex has been downregulated.

Viveka is a natural awareness we all have, but it is suppressed from our overegotistical control. Viveka can be a state of perceiving the inner world only when our mind has undergone *nirodha,* which in Sanskrit means "stillness" and the "settling of the mind." If we allow the mind to settle into stillness more often, we will develop viveka, which in turn will train the cold cognition to be less sticky and more receptive to the spontaneous virtue of the unconscious. In downregulating the "I" we begin to see reality as it truly is without blocking the stream of the universe. This has long-term effects.

BRINGING HOT COGNITION TO LIFE

Bringing the stream of the universe forward cannot be achieved only by the hot system at the expense of the cold system. As I have mentioned, the two systems have to be integrated, though we should not overcompensate for the cold cognitive regions. Cold cognition should be like a lighthouse that scans the environment objectively. When we identify with the environment as good or bad then we are led into suffering from the illusion of the separation of self and other.

We cannot be totally one without the other, but we can overuse the cold function, which leads to many of the problems that I've mentioned. However, cold cognition can be beneficial in establishing frameworks for hot cognition to express universal beauty. For example, when we are learning an art, let's say music, we go through years of rigorous training that depend on the focus of your cold cognitive controls. But after these years of training, and once you have assimilated the framework, then you can let the music of the universe explode through you without having to think about it, because the sense of "I" doesn't get in the way. It is just like riding a bike; the skill is ingrained. The idea of the person is not there and instead an intelligent spontaneity takes over, what the Chinese call the effortlessness of wu-wei. As Edward Slingerland states:

> "We" tend to identify with the cold, slow system because it is the seat of our conscious awareness and our sense of self. Beneath this conscious self, though, is another self—much bigger and more powerful—that we have no direct access to. It is this deeper, more evolutionarily ancient part of us that knows how to spit and move our legs around. It's also the part that we are struggling with when we try to resist that tiramisu or drag ourselves out of bed for an important meeting.
>
> The goal of *wu-wei* is to get these two selves working together smoothly and effectively. For a person in *wu-wei*, the mind is embodied and the body is mindful; the two systems—hot and cold, fast and slow—are completely integrated. The result is an intelligent spontaneity that is perfectly calibrated to the environment.[5]

Hot cognition expresses itself virtuously through frameworks of understanding, for example, the fact that I know the alphabet and the structures of sentences, which allow me to write this book. Cultivating certain disciplines, on the other hand, like meditative practices, will settle the mind down to allow a samskara-free hot cognition to manifest through your consciousness. This will have an effect on your spontaneous reactions to the world, and eventually become the intelligent spontaneity of Cook Ting.

In practicing meditation, open awareness or otherwise, we are accessing the parasympathetic nervous system, which eventually effects our enteric nervous system (ENS). The enteric nervous system is a meshlike network of neurons that governs the function of the gastrointestinal system, known more commonly as our gut instincts. Our gut instincts come from the enteric nervous system and can be tuned in to by downregulating the sense of "I." We hear messages from the gut more clearly and louder, and we can essentially act in accord with spontaneous reactions and judgment calls. We begin to move as though we can sense the universe's future we are about to experience. But all that has really happened is our enteric nervous system is functioning without the hindrance of the prefrontal cortex and is aligned with the environment like Cook Ting.

This is our nature when we downregulate the cold cognitive regions of the mind. As a result we bring forth the magic within the unconscious hot cognition to life. Artists and athletes have this ability because they allow the hot processes of the mind to come forth, even though most are not conscious of this. Sages also perfect this mind, as they bring the wisdom of the universe forth, but they are aware that this cannot happen if they hold on to the idea of themselves as a separate person. Letting go of this idea is not simple, since we are taught to uphold it. To transcend the prison of the ego and bring the spontaneous virtue of the universe forward, we first need to learn the discipline and techniques of mind fasting.

7

THE ART OF
PRACTICING
MIND FASTING

Fasting the mind is easier said than done. It requires immense discipline and a transformation of your lifestyle. But paradoxically it is not hard at all; it is the easiest thing in the world to accomplish because your true nature is an empty liberated mind. The enlightenment we seek is not really an event at all, nor is it a place to get to. The real liberation is in ceasing our search, because essentially in giving up searching we find what we've always been, and this is paradoxically what we've been searching for. It has been right under our noses all along. The reason we don't see it is because the illusion of a separate isolated personality blurs our vision. It is actually our personality that believes fasting the mind is "easier said than done," because the whole discipline is aimed at the dissolution of that personality.

Our original nature is pure and liberated, which can never be anywhere but *now* because it is the eternal essence of the universe, the Atman, which is Brahman. (I explore this concept in depth in my book *Enlightenment Now.*) We believe only that we're not liberated when we live in the impermanence and limitations of the personality, which is a construct of samsara, that is, of time.

Fasting the mind is essentially an ancient art of healing to bring you back to the present moment where you've always been in reality, but the illusion of past and future have clouded this reality. It is a map to nowhere, meaning "now here." To be able to follow this map to *now* paradoxically requires effort and the discipline of mind fasting. This curious paradox of being liberated eternally and at the same time bound to time is the central focus of Zen Buddhism, such as when they speak of the perfection of Zen, or that we're always in nirvana now in the midst of samsara time. Austrian-born American physicist Fritjof Capra explains this paradox found in Zen Buddhism in his book *The Tao of Physics:*

> The perfection of Zen is thus to live one's everyday life naturally and spontaneously. When Po-chang was asked to define Zen, he said, "When hungry eat, when tired sleep." Although this sounds simple and obvious, like so much in Zen, it is in fact quite a difficult task. To regain the naturalness of our original nature requires long train-ing and constitutes a great spiritual achievement. In the words of a famous Zen saying,
>
> *Before you study Zen, mountains are mountains and rivers are riv-ers; while you are studying Zen, mountains are no longer mountains and rivers are no longer rivers; but once you have had enlightenment, mountains are once again mountains and rivers again rivers.*
>
> Zen's emphasis on naturalness and spontaneity certainly shows its Taoist roots, but the basis for this emphasis is strictly Buddhistic. It is the belief in the perfection of our original nature, the realization that the process of enlightenment consists merely in becoming what we already are from the beginning.[1]

Our original nature is spontaneously natural in the eternal now, as Capra explained. The practice of fasting the mind is to clear the dust from our mental window so that the rays of the eternal Brahman Sun can shine through us without being obstructed. Once the mind has completely fasted, we come back into our original enlightened nature to live in accord to the world with an unstuck effortless mind. This ease we feel in life from a liberated mind is the real enlightenment that was evident in the consciousness of the great sages, Gautama the Buddha for example. This is what I call Zen in life.

ZEN IN LIFE

Indian spiritual guru and yoga adept Swami Satchidananda once said that enlightenment was not some fantastic event, but rather it is an ease we feel when we have stepped out of the murk of the personality and into the light of God. This is how the awareness of enlightenment is commonly understood in the East. But in the West enlightenment has been misinterpreted as more like a Hollywood epic that we will experience once we have suffered enough to gain it. Enlightenment is no event or place to reach, as the sages of the East sufficiently explained. It is as Swami Satchidananda explained, an ease we feel in every moment of life, yet this ease is beyond relaxation.

This ease comes because the contracted aspect of consciousness we know as "I" has been downregulated. This frees us to live in the world without being a prisoner to our personality's perception of the world. We see things as they truly *are* without labeling or naming the experience and what we are experiencing. Essentially Zen in life is Zen in every moment. Becoming one who is completely liberated in this life, which in Sanskrit is called a jivanmukta, is the goal of fasting the mind, but the goal is not somewhere or something you reach; it is more a recognition of what was always true. The mind eventually fasts so completely that you give away the practice or discipline because you have reached its objective, which is to live from that spontaneously natural awareness in this eternal moment. This is the goal of many Eastern wisdom traditions: the recognition that you were always enlightened.

The purpose of living a monastic life or staying in a monastery or ashram for a period of time is to realize enlightenment right now, which paradoxically can only be experienced in a prolonged state if we fast the mind. Likewise with spiritual practices such as hatha yoga or t'ai chi, the key is to realize your enlightened eternal nature. It is definitely beneficial to practice an art of spiritual cultivation or spend a lot of time in a monastery, but eventually you need to walk Zen in life. To live the purpose of a spiritual practice or spiritual clinic is to be Zen in every moment of life where you will bring much-needed spiritual oxygen to the world so it can begin to breathe again rather than drown in the suffocation of identity. Being Zen in life happens when you drop the striving and free yourself, seeing that the constructs of the linear world have been exposed as an illusion that has kept you away from the nonlinear now. Being Zen in life is a pure lifestyle. It's not just about meditation or having a meditative mind. Rather, it means your life itself becomes meditation in the sense that your perceptions disappear so you can experience the nondual innate beauty of life without the illusionary confusion of separate opposites.

Fasting the mind is the common medicine found in the East to clean our perceptions to free us to walk Zen in life. But as I mentioned earlier, fasting the mind is not just meditation; it is also about starving the mind from our habitual comforts that tend to distract us. What distracts us is what we seek to fast away so our entire life can be transformed. To be sure meditation is a part of this, but it is what we take in through the nine gates of the five senses that are required to cleanse the sixth sense.

PURIFYING EATING HABITS

The most pervasive way we seek to distract ourselves is through what we eat and drink. People often talk about "comfort food," as if it really brings us comfort. In general, comfort food is bad for you because it often involves foods high in sugar and starch that we indulge in, like sweets, when we are sad to try to cheer us up. But eating such foods only suppresses the pain, keeping you from actually dealing with it—all the while causing you to become physically unhealthy as a result.

We often mask our psychological pain by eating snacks and over-indulging in what we eat and drink, which causes unnecessary agitation in the mind and nervous system. To counter this agitation we need to be conscious of our psychological pain and stay with it rather than push it away. The only way to heal our pain, as we've discussed, is to be conscious of it, which begins the deep healing process. Only then can we realize how toxic is the food that we've been putting in our mouths. Being unaware of the food we eat can cause a lot of damage to our psychosomatic organism. This unaware attitude is the response of a lazy and unconscious mind. I am not going to suggest a particular diet to follow—such as vegan, vegetarian, paleo, primal, ketogenic, or ayurveda—except to say that a disciplined diet is essential in fasting the mind because it changes one of our fundamental habits, which we tend to take for granted. Following a disciplined diet will change your eating habits and give you some focus. But your diet may also change over time as you become more conscious of your bodily needs.

Many people erroneously believe there is only one correct diet for everyone. But biologically everybody is different, and everyone has different responses to particular foods—something that is explained by the three body types, or *doshas,* in Indian ayurveda: *pitta, vata,* and *kapha.* In addition, not everybody can have the same diet due to environmental factors. For example, the Inuit people have limited sources of food.

Nevertheless, it is important to choose a healthy diet that works for you. Changing your eating habits through a disciplined diet begins to transform the mind's familiar lazy tendencies, which results in a fundamental change at the samskara level. Having a disciplined diet helps reduce weight and leads to better health, because you will train yourself not to reach for the next candy bar, for example. The particular diet doesn't matter so much as the self-discipline to refrain from foods that lead to bad health.

Essential to mind fasting is reducing those foods that subtly agitate the mind—which is a signal that this stuff is terrible for us. Reducing refined sugars, refined wheat, and caffeine is essential. These three are highly addictive and have become the core of our industrial diets. Refined sugar, for example, acts like a drug that many people consume daily, becoming addicted to products such as Coca-Cola. Excessive sugar consumption causes damage to the body and mind, and is believed to lead to dementia, especially Alzheimer's disease. American neurologist and Fellow of the American College of Nutrition Dr. David Perlmutter explains sugars connection to Alzheimer's and two simple lifestyle choices to reduce the risk of this disease:

> While our government invests millions of dollars in finding a pharmaceutical to prevent Alzheimer's, study after study has continued to find evidence that through slight variations in our daily diet as well as dedication to exercise, we can have a marked effect on reducing our risk for Alzheimer's as well as actually improve brain performance. Studies have come out linking increased blood sugar with a reduction in the size of the hippocampus, the brain's memory center. What does this mean? It means we shouldn't be surprised to learn that predicted growth in the number of Americans with Type 2 Diabetes is coupled with similar growth in the number of Americans expected to be diagnosed with Alzheimer's in the coming decades.[2]

Unrefined sugars are much less harmful, however, particularly if consumed in moderation. But refined sugars, particularly refined fructose, have found their way into many of today's processed foods and drinks, from pasta sauce to milk. It is this refined variety of sugar we should avoid at all costs.

As for refined wheat, it does not contribute to physical or mental health if taken excessively. Gluten, a mixture of proteins found in wheat and other related grains, is something to avoid in the mind-fasting process and for our all-around brain health. Dr. David Perlmutter explains the health issues concerning gluten:

> Gluten is a foreign protein to human physiology, and is the cornerstone of leaky brain—causing inflammation. Science has made some amazing discoveries about the blood brain barrier in recent years, most importantly that it can become just as permeable as our gut lining. When gluten is introduced to the body, it turns out that inflammation that degrades this important barrier.[3]

To give an example of the effects of refined flour and sugar, the consumption of both has increased dramatically per person in India over the past few hundred years, which may have been influenced by the British resulting from their processing methods when they governed the Indian subcontinent. (India is the second-largest producer of sugarcane and the third largest producer of wheat. Keep in mind the European Union is first when it comes to wheat production, which means if we went by individual nations, India is second when it comes to wheat.[4]) This has become a real concern in India, considering the now-typical Hindu vegetarian diet consists of a lot of refined sugar and flour and not many vegetables. As a result India has one of the highest rates of diabetes in the world, not to mention high obesity and a bunch of other diseases from refined flour.

As with refined sugar and flour, caffeine has become so habitual in the modern diet that many people do not know that they are literally high for much of the day. The excessive coffee consumption we see today leads to the jitteriness that many people often feel. People are constantly fidgeting and chronically agitated from the speed and intensity that excessive caffeine produces. This does nothing but depletes the energy of the nervous system, which exhausts the mind. It is hard to communicate with people who are constantly on the drug of caffeine. It is such an intense stimulant for their mind that they are not themselves due to mental exhaustion. In ancient health practices, such as traditional Chinese medicine, coffee is understood to have little, if any, value as a food. Brendan Kelly, an American Chinese medical practitioner, explains the symptoms of coffee consumption and how coffee contributes to excessive heat (yang) in the body in his book *The Yin and Yang of Climate Crisis*:

> For many of us, drinking coffee can produce a long list of symptoms . . . and can contribute to, or create, a wide range of [others], including anxiety, racing thoughts, insomnia, disturbed dreams, headaches (including migraines), acid reflux, irritable bowel syndrome, a wide range of stomach and intestinal issues, fibroids of all kinds, (including uterine fibroids), growths of all kinds (including tumors), a wide range of skin conditions including eczema, arthritis, a wide range of pain conditions (including fibromyalgia), heart palpitations, excess anger and aggression, dizziness and vertigo, lower-back and leg weakness and pain, a lack of rooted energy in general. In fact, all chronic and acute conditions that involve heat from the Chinese perspective and inflammation from the Western perspective are likely exacerbated by coffee.[5]

Holistic physicians believe coffee is better suited for enemas than ingestion through the mouth. I guess something that works efficiently for our bowels is going to have an interesting effect when we ingest it. But even with enemas, the effects of coffee are still absorbed in the body, causing an agitated response. As a result its health benefits are questionable. A healthier alternative to coffee is tea, especially if it is caffeine free. But even regular tea contains so little caffeine that it won't agitate your mind like coffee does, and has more of a calming effect. As with anything else, consume tea in moderation. It cannot hurt to cut out coffee altogether if you are focused on fasting the mind.

Moderation is a key ingredient for fasting the mind. Keeping our diets simple and not overindulging will naturally settle the activity and movement of the mind. Reducing our intake of food should be imperative. When we bombard the stomach with excessive food consumption our internal organs have to work overtime to try to digest everything we keep putting in. This naturally causes agitation in the mind, as the organs and the mind are linked. When we reduce our food intake with three simple meals a day, and with no snacking in between, then the digestive system functions naturally without being overdriven, which ultimately leads to an equanimous mind. This is why people feel great when they physically detox or fast because the digestive system has slowed down.

Moderation is also why monasteries and ashrams often serve only two small meals a day: breakfast and lunch. It is linked to the clarity of mind needed for the extensive meditation that is practiced in an ashram or monastery. It also breaks the habit of eating too much. Monasteries and ashrams are attempting to influence your lives with this mind-fasting technique. Reducing our intake should be one of our daily practices for fasting the mind. This practice brings our biology back in accord with nature, and we begin to listen to what the body truly needs without our mind craving stimulation. Returning to nature brings us to the last aspect of purifying our eating habits.

When we fast the mind, eliminating processed foods is imperative. I know that may appear hard because of how our culture is inundated with processed foods, but it truly isn't that hard when you remove distractions and reclaim your time. The reason we should eliminate processed foods is because, just like refined sugar, flour, and caffeine, they agitate the mind on a subtle level. This is why you will not find any processed foods at monasteries or ashrams. Besides, processed foods are not a healthy alternative to real foods. Consuming too many processed foods leads us to crave them more and more, because in many cases they are infused with fructose, gluten, and caffeine. This tension of craving overshadows our awareness of what really good food is.

Processed food is a product of our modern culture, which is programmed toward comfort and convenience. We are increasingly becoming lazy and our food is an instant creation of thought from our get-it-now culture, which resembles a pig trough more than a plate of human food. If we fast our mind from the distractions of the world we will naturally be attracted to real wholesome food, and with fewer distractions, we will have more time to prepare better food. Instead of buying a sauce at the supermarket, for example, we have the time to make our own sauce with natural ingredients, which actually taste better. Returning to a natural diet goes hand in hand with fasting the mind. The reason for this return to nature is because the mind returns to its own nature, which is emptiness. This return to nature is not just in the food we consume through our mouth, but also through the "food" we take in through our eyes and ears.

DIGITAL DETOX

If you are constantly using a digital device, phone, computer, television, and so on, there is no chance for your mind to reach equanimity. It is just impossible. For example, how many of you have used a digital device before bed, but then toss and turn for hours? That's right—many people who read this have had that same experience at least once. In recent times our sleeping patterns are out of sync as a result of too much digital stimulation. People are sleeping less and insomnia is on the increase because people are addicted to the drug of digital devices.

According to Taoism, engaging in *yang* (masculine/active) activities at night will cause you to be out of sync with nature, because nighttime is time for *yin* (feminine/receptive) energy, when we are supposed to rest and shut down our sense activity. If you engage in yang activities at night your mind becomes agitated and ready for action because it thinks it is the beginning of the day when yang is naturally high. This is why we become restless when we try to sleep at night. Our mind is moving at a time when it should be resting.

To articulate how absurd this is, just imagine waking up at 6 a.m. after a good eight hours of sleep. You have breakfast at 7 a.m., wash the dishes, and prepare to go to bed at 8 a.m. Sounds ridiculous, right? Well, this is what we are essentially doing when we are on digital devices at nighttime. As we cannot repeat the flow of the day with yin and then yin, so we cannot have yang followed by yang. Daytime, not nighttime, is for the creative aspect of yang. As I mentioned earlier, most of us are not more popular than Christopher Nolan. If he can get by without an e-mail account or a mobile phone, then I'm sure we don't need to check these devices at nighttime, if at all. When fasting the mind a digital detox is essential, as the mind has no chance of nirodha (stillness) if it is constantly stimulated. We need to have methods of countering the digital bombardment if we are to cultivate our natural empty mind.

If you are not so lucky to live without the need of a phone, computer, or television, then efficient methods need to be practiced daily. One such method is "digital sunsets." *Digital sunset* was a phrase coined by American philosopher and optimal life coach Brian Johnson to eliminate the problem of using digital devices and watching regular television at nighttime. Shut down all your digital devices around 6 p.m., or, even better, 5 p.m.; maybe then we will learn to talk to each other face-to-face, eye to eye again. Practicing digital sunsets eliminates our habit of using digital devices at night. This method also follows nature because the blue light in digital devices disrupts the natural function of our pineal gland. Scientific research has revealed that the pineal gland—a pea-size organ in the brain that French philosopher, mathematician, and scientist René Descartes believed to be the "principal seat of the soul"— begins to release melatonin (a hormone produced in the pineal gland that regulates biological rhythms) a few hours before your regular bedtime, which reduces your alertness and makes sleep more inviting. But exposure to blue light at nighttime can keep the pineal gland from secreting melatonin and ultimately mess with our circadian rhythms, affecting our sleep patterns.*

---

*For more on the relationship between sleep, the pineal gland, and blue light see the following articles: "The Role of Melatonin in the Circadian Rhythm Sleep-Wake Cycle," by Atul Khullar, www.psychiatrictimes.com/sleep-disorders/role-melatonin-circadian-rhythm-sleep-wake-cycle; "Blue Light Has a Dark Side," from Harvard Health Publications, www.health.harvard.edu/staying-healthy/blue-light-has-a-dark-side; and "Seeing Blue: The Impact of Excessive Blue Light Exposure," by Heather Flint Ford, www.reviewofoptometry.com/article/seeing-blue-the-impact-of-excessive-blue-light-exposure.

Practicing the digital-sunset method literally preserves our brain's health, providing biological evidence of the benefits of fasting the mind. When you practice digital sunsets for a long time you will feel your mind and nervous system begin to be more calm and relaxed, even at daytime. Sleep becomes deeper and easier to fall into. Just this simple practice will do a lot to transform your lifestyle. The more time we spend away from digital screens, the more we come back into resonance with nature and her cyclical rhythm.

Our mind is not agitated and distracted as a result of a digital detox. We finally become responsible for what we consume through our eyes and ears. When we don't consume copious amounts of noise our mind does not accumulate more samskaras and it becomes easier to deal with the damage already done on the subtle level of the samskaras. In addressing both our food diet and digital diet we confront what we unconsciously consume that invariably distracts our mind from its natural presence. A return to the natural order of life (that is, to the Tao) is to realize our innate presence within an empty and fasted mind. Residing within the order of life, we recognize that nature is intrinsically simple until our mind confuses this with labels and interpretations. When we fast the mind we realize that our mind can also be simple, because it is empty of name and form—just like nature, because it is nature.

KEEP IT SIMPLE, STUPID

The practice of fasting the mind to transform our lifestyle should abide by the KISS method. KISS is an acronym for a common phrase we are familiar with: "Keep it simple, stupid." Now, I'm not saying you're stupid, but instead I am saying that we are stupid when we bombard the mind with complexity, which leads us into a stupefied state. Our lifestyle must be simplified. So many of the mental diseases and problems in our culture arise from consuming mental complexity, which in the end confuses us because, amazingly, we identify with its complex contents. From becoming conscious of what we consume through the nine gates we simplify our lives. But when we seek out complexity, we turn away from our true simple nature—and that's the stupid part of "keep it simple, stupid."

As with everything else we have mentioned about fasting the mind, our personality needs to be downregulated and this can be achieved in our lifestyle with a discipline every day to simplify our habits, just like with our food and digital diets. Our lifestyle essentially has to be basic.

To get back to a basic lifestyle we have to approach every day as a piece of art. Each day can be a masterpiece or a disaster, depending on whether you have practiced mind fasting in your life or not. When we fast the mind our lifestyle becomes basic, as the complex components of distraction are weeded out. As with any artist, to achieve a masterpiece one must be firm in the basics, with an ability to empty one's mind so that there is no distinction between artist and art. It is the same for living masterpiece days. The art of living mind fasting in our lifestyle is about getting back to the basics. Then every day can be a masterpiece day. What do we essentially need?

There are four fundamentals that are essential for manifesting a masterpiece day: meditation, exercise, healthy diet, and adequate rest, in no particular order. These four fundamentals should be evenly distributed, not in time but in energy. We should not overcompensate for one at the expense of another. Many people do this, particularly in regard to rest. They live an excessively active life but do not get adequate rest, leading to all sorts of psychological problems.

Without adequate rest the three remaining fundamentals suffer. It is essential to let our nervous system completely shut down every day for at least seven hours, but eight hours is better for anyone to be functioning at an optimal level of well-being. However, if we do consistently get adequate rest our life becomes extremely vibrant as we tap into an unbridled enthusiasm for anything life offers, which enhances our productivity naturally in a nonegotistical manner. Sleep is the power base for the other three fundamentals. If we consistently get enough sleep the energy distribution allocated for the other three fundamentals is optimal. As a result our meditation practice becomes deeper and more vivid with the ability to silence the mind for longer periods of time. We will also have more energy for consistent exercise routines as well as more enthusiasm for regularly eating healthy food.

Following these four fundamental fasting-the-mind lifestyle disciplines will give you a firm foundation in your everyday experience that will naturally evoke health, well-being, and the secret element of creativity.

THE CREATIVE ART OF LIFE

We achieve health and well-being by following these four fundamental disciplines, which are the fertile mental soil for creativity. If we keep a healthy balance of meditation, exercise, healthy diet, and rest every day, then this will settle our mind naturally so we can begin to hear our intuition crying out for creative expression. This does not mean that we then begin to overcompensate for creativity. But instead our natural creative expression (li) becomes the hidden fifth element of our masterpiece day that we learn not to be anxious about, which is often the problem for many artists. Instead of overindulging in creativity as a result of the fundamental four disciplines, we begin to practice "time blocking," rather than giving our creativity the lion's share of the time in our day. *Time blocking* means "dedicating a set amount of time to creative work," rather than trying to do the creative activities all the time.

For example, in writing this book I practiced time blocking consistently every day, except for time off during weekends, for two months. On top of the disciplines of the four basic fundamental elements of mind fasting, I wrote from 8:30 a.m. to 12:30 p.m., using that period as my time block during which the creative juices would flow. Using this time-blocking practice for my writing allowed me to remain focused on my work like never before. Yet this consistency and energy for my own creative expression could not be achieved if I lost my daily rhythm of meditation, exercise, healthy diet, and adequate rest. This is the same with anybody, because our psychosomatic organism has generally the same makeup when it comes to daily energy and rhythm.

To find your rhythm you should not be confused into thinking there is a particular meditative technique, exercise routine, or diet to follow, in just the same way that a lot of you reading this book will have a different creative expression from mine. In this book I have mentioned two ancient meditative techniques, vipassana and Zen (open awareness), simple yet advanced practices that you could follow. But on top of these there are so many great techniques out there. Likewise with exercise and diet, each psychosomatic constitution is different and we should find our own nature and rhythm in that regard. But in most respects fasting the mind should be the primary focus in meditation, exercise, and diet, and also with creativity.

It's easy to assume that creative people sit around coffee shops, chatting and occasionally writing something down on paper, if they were a writer, for example. As a writer I can tell you nothing could be farther from the truth. In general creative people live a relatively boring life, according to others, but it is not boring from their perspective. What may seem like a boring life is actually a breeding ground for pure creative expression. By following the basic four mind-fasting disciplines, we enter this relatively unknown field of creative expression. This daily rhythm is the art of life, or the art of living according to Lao-tzu. The art of life comes alive through your own organic creative expression in the depths of your consciousness.

Yet, as with the four fundamentals, our creativity can get out of balance if it becomes a mental game that we obsess about. Habitual obsessing disrupts our mind's equanimity, and our life in general. Creativity should not be something that we excessively think about and do for the rewards we may attain from it. On the contrary, creativity is the art of life, blossoming through a mind that has fasted. And here I mean pure, dedicated, creative expression, which takes discipline to master—not just someone doodling on a piece of paper for fun. Real creativity is born in an empty mind, and in actual fact is a method for fasting the mind. To realize this is to recognize that the harmonious rhythm of our daily life is not complete if creativity is not a discipline. Doing creative work itself is a practice for fasting the mind. Making creativity a deliberate practice forces the ego-mind out of its lazy comfort zones.

People who enjoy creative work and put a lot of effort into it make their life a living art form through fasting the mind during the process. The reason we live in an uncreative world is because in general people are distracted. A mind full of noise can never be truly creative. An example of this is when we observe people who set out to be creative or achieve a task and they lack the ability to focus for more than five minutes—and even five minutes is a generous estimate! What often happens at the five-minute mark is their mind tries to run away from the effort required for the task by seeking any sort of distraction. People often say to me that they are attracted to writing creatively, but when they sit at their computer to write they have all of their social media and e-mail windows open, which distract the mind. As a result they constantly check these windows to get away from the effort needed to be creative. As I mentioned earlier, none of us is so popular that we must check e-mail, Facebook, and Twitter all the time. This is one reason I write with pen and paper first, because I understand the mind's petty little games.

A great strategy for fasting the mind during a creative discipline is what is known as deep work. American professor of computer science Cal Newport formalized a dedicated creative discipline that has for the most part been isolated to writers and philosophers. He explores this kind of creative dedication, for which he coined with the phrase *deep work,* in his book aptly titled *Deep Work.* According to Newport, creative dedication minus distractions equals high productivity, which is the goal of deep work. Deep work is the discipline of focused attention for long periods of time without being distracted. Newport explains deep work in this manner:

Professional activities performed in a state of distraction-free concentration that push cognitive capabilities to their limit. These
efforts create new value, improve your skill, and are hard to
replicate.[6]

Newport's hypothesis is that deep work is becoming the most valuable commodity in our current economic climate, especially among
the growing field of knowledge workers in the world. He explains
further:

Deep work is not some nostalgic affection of writers and early-
twentieth-century philosophers. It's instead a skill that has great
value today.[7]

I would take this one step farther and state that deep work is valuable to not just knowledge workers, but also athletes, artists, and almost
anybody who is trying to cultivate a discipline to fast the mind. This
discipline is nothing new and it is actually similar to the temperament
of vipassana meditation and Zen Buddhism that we mentioned earlier,
especially if you spend extensive time in a monastery. The discipline
of deep work, as well as the traditions of vipassana, Zen, and Vedanta,
to name just a few, is about focusing the mind on a single point of
activity without letting your mind drift off into habitual distractions.
You essentially give your entire being to each activity in each moment.
Doesn't this sound very similar to meditation? Well, that's because in
essence it is, as the principle is the same.

Yet deep work is not some new commodity, as Cal Newport pointed
out. In times gone by deep work was thought of as essential for developing any skill through the meditative practice of sustained focused attention. Though this may appeal to the modern-day individual, the real
depth of the practice is still often missing.

Deep work in the modern day is thought of solely as an exercise
to achieve results. Our success-driven culture misses the point of such

practices, as we focus on ends and conclusions. The modern practice of deep work becomes, then, about achieving these ends at the expense of seeing the intrinsic value of the process. Focusing on linear ends and demands at the expense of the nonlinear process of eternal becoming is the hallmark of our modern materialist culture. This is completely different from the attitude of the ancient original proponents of deep work. Many artists and writers will explain that it is the process they enjoy more than the end result. As with a dance, we know it is the dance itself that is beautiful, but we find it difficult to extend this truth into our immediate life. But the original deep-work practitioners were in touch with this beauty through the process of their craft, whatever that may be.

In ancient times deep work was a method for fasting the mind. Unlike some other mind-fasting strategies, this method requires concentration on a task to begin with, rather than just emptying the mind. The result of focused attention on a task is the same cognitively when we practice meditation. Many people in the modern world know nothing about this method or the state of consciousness that arises from the process because their minds are filled with noise from distractions, causing them to constantly seek even more distraction.

When we put our awareness on a certain aspect of the inner world in meditation—sensations, for example—we slowly enter the effortless natural state that is ever present within our hot cognition. When we sit down, disconnect from distractions, and focus on the job at hand, if we can maintain that focus for a long period of time we enter the effortlessness of wu-wei without trying to induce it. Sustained focus, then, evokes naturalness. And when we are in this state, the sense of our persona, our "I," has been downregulated, and as a result the universal will expresses itself through you, as yourself but without any blockage. Through the constant practice of deep work in our creative life we step beyond ourselves to serve something much greater than our personality.

TO SERVE THE WORLD WE MUST
FAST THE MIND

Many people try to serve the world according to their own beliefs and values. But history tells us that this in no way serves the world. With this mind-set we are actually only interfering with the world, trying to impose our will over others on a subtle level. But if we seek to fast the mind, our entire lifestyle begins to serve something greater than our personal ego-mind. Being Zen in our entire life affects even our creative expression through the process of deep work. As a result, the personal egotistical mind is transcended as we cultivate sustained focus minus distractions. We need to always keep in mind that distractions are the hallmark of the lazy ego.

When we operate on the deep level, we have fasted the personal mind away and begin to serve something much greater than ourselves. That which is greater can be anything, because the point is that you serve something that is neither self-interested nor seeking reward or benefit. It is, rather, an act of surrender to that which is greater than yourself. Now, don't assume that this means an act of surrender to God, though it can mean that for some people. But for others it can mean surrendering to their particular creative expression or craft. The point is that you surrender to that which is beyond your distracted ego-mind and as a result you serve the world authentically from this process. Some artists give their entire life to their craft, which serves the world in an indirect manner. Yet they cannot do this in a distracted state. They must fast their mind through the process of disciplined creative expression, or deep work. Whether artists know this consciously is debatable, and in some sense not important if they have surrendered humbly to their craft. So it doesn't matter if you surrender to God or to your creative life; the point is that the act of surrender itself is the divine principle of the universe that brings the light of inspiration into the world.

The bodhisattvas of ancient times surrendered their entire minds to the dharma teachings of Gautama the Buddha, which is an act of serving something greater than oneself. One of the essential principles of a bodhisattva is that when we completely fast the mind so that it returns to its original purity, we paradoxically become useful without any intention to do so. Until then we are not useful but are instead only a nuisance. Those who truly want to wake up will recognize that many in this modern world are stuck in this nuisance state.

OVERCOMING THE OBSTACLES OF DAILY LIFE

Many people assume that the practice of fasting the mind is far too difficult and not practical in daily life. This assumption in a sense is a cop-out. First of all, nothing is more natural and easy than fasting the mind, because that is our original nature of mind. The real problem— and ironically why we think fasting the mind is so difficult—is that we have become accustomed to the lazy habits and tendencies of the ego-mind. We are so used to distracting ourselves that anything other than distraction seems unattainable. This is because in our daily life we encounter so many obstacles that it feels easier to just fall back into distraction, back in line with the common attitude of the social world.

We believe it is just easier to succumb to the ways of the world, but this choice leaves us feeling empty inside with no real contentment. If we are sincere about the mind's equanimity, world peace, and the complete liberation of the individual, then we need to cultivate methods that will support our practice of fasting the mind in daily life. We essentially have to cultivate skills that will give us the awareness to overcome any obstacle.

To achieve this we need to set the conditions for our life so it can begin to bear fruit. To use an athlete as an example, they do everything possible to lay the groundwork for a peak performance. This means they set the conditions to favor positive outcomes. In their field this means training their butts off, eating well, analyzing the strategy of their sport, and getting a lot of rest. If they can maintain this rhythm, then it can be fertile soil for growth. In the same way, when we examine fasting the mind—or any spiritual practice or doctrine for that matter—the rhythm and art of life we seek is to *be* Zen in life.

Yet to be in this natural state of mind requires us to set the conditions for the great fast. Following the methods of the science of healing the framework of samsara—downregulating the sense of "I," purifying our eating habits, detoxing from digital devices, sticking to the four fundamentals of keeping it simple (meditation, healthy diet, exercise, adequate rest), and maintaining an undistracted creative life—are the foundations for keeping the mind in a state of Zen, meaning "being empty," but also in a state of effortless motion with no deliberation.

On top of this foundation we need to nourish our immediate daily life. In the East it is essential to work from the ground up when we speak about fasting the mind. This means we begin with the consecration of our home. Setting the conditions for an equanimous mind begins with transforming your home into a living temple. In China this is called feng shui, which is the art of bringing harmony to one's life. Feng shui is about setting the conditions for harmony, and that is most important in your home because it eventually helps promote the well-being of your immediate relationships.

India also has a tradition of consecrating the home, which is heavily advocated by the Indian spiritual teacher Sadhguru Jaggi Vasudev. In India almost every home has a *puja* (Hindu for "worship") shrine in a designated room. Consecrating the home has been a tradition in both China and India for thousands of years. The art of consecrating your home will set the conditions for fasting the mind, as home life becomes more about meditation and harmonious relationships than anything to do with distractions.

When many people step out of their home life and into work and society, they face unforeseen obstacles, many of which conflict with the practice of fasting the mind. Yet it doesn't have to be that way. We need to actually develop skills to overcome such obstacles. In the chaos and craziness of life that is India, the use of mantras (sacred utterances, numinous sounds, or groups of words believed to have psychological or spiritual power) are extremely useful for maintaining a fasted mind. Anyone who has visited India will know it can be the most sacred and beautiful place on the planet, but at the same time one of the busiest and frustrating places on Earth. Indian people know this best, and use mantras as a holy sacrament to deal with this paradox.

Reciting mantras plays a large role in many of India's religious activities, such as the circumambulation of the holy mountain of Arunachala. In the southern Indian city of Tiruvannamalai, best known for the great sage Sri Ramana Maharshi and the holy mountain of Arunachala, people descend on this small town for a sacred day known as Karthikai Deepam. On this day millions arrive in this small city to walk barefoot clockwise around Arunachala, which is thought to be a manifestation of Shiva. On full-moon days—or almost any day, for that matter—you can see people making the long walk around Arunachala. The circumambulation of Arunachala (known as *Giri Pradakshina* in Sanskrit and *Giri Valam* in Tamil) covers a distance of 14 kilometers (8.7 miles). The common theme on all days is to constantly recite the mantra *Om Namah Shivaya* to keep their mind fasted and free from distracting thoughts. *Om Namah Shivaya* actually means "adoration to Shiva," or, for English speakers, "adoration to God." Shiva is the destructive or transformational principle of the *Trimurti* (the three Hindu gods: Brahma the creator, Vishnu the preserver, and Shiva the destroyer or transformer). Since Shiva personifies the function of the universe that destroys or transforms the ego, he is associated to the element of fire.

A similar tradition can be found in the small town of Bodh Gaya in the northern Indian state of Bihar. Bodh Gaya is home to the famous Bodhi tree, where the historical Buddha, Guatama the Buddha, attained enlightenment. Around the tree has been built the Mahabodhi Temple. Nowadays Buddhists and numerous people from around the world make the slow, mindful walk around the Bodhi tree and the Mahabodhi Temple while they recite certain mantras or Buddhist texts. One of the more common mantras that people recite is *Om mani padme hum,* which is often interpreted as "jewel in the lotus flower." This mantra is found carved into rocks in thousands if not millions of places in northern India, Nepal, and Tibet. The fourteenth Dalai Lama explains the significance of this mantra:

> It is very good to recite the mantra OM MANI PADME HUM, but while you are doing it, you should be thinking on its meaning, for the meaning of the six syllables is great and vast. The first, OM, is composed of three pure letters, A, U, and M. These symbolize the practitioner's impure body, speech, and mind; they also symbolize the pure exalted body, speech, and mind of a Buddha. [. . .]
>
> The path is indicated by the next four syllables. MANI, meaning jewel, symbolizes the factor of method—the altruistic intention to become enlightened, compassion, and love. [. . .]
>
> The two syllables, PADME, meaning lotus, symbolize wisdom. [. . .]
>
> Purity must be achieved by an indivisible unity of method and wisdom, symbolized by the final syllable, HUM, which indicates indivisibility. [. . .]
>
> Thus the six syllables, OM MANI PADME HUM, mean that in dependence on the practice which is an indivisible union of method and wisdom, you can transform your impure body, speech, and mind into the pure body, speech, and mind of a Buddha.[8]

Both of these mantras—*Om Namah Shivaya* and *Om mani padme hum*—are actually among the more common mantras for Hindus and Buddhists. I mention both of these mantras because they are actually mind tools. In fact, the word *mantra* is the combination of two Sanskrit words: *manas,* which means "mind"; and *tra,* which means "tool." So it's better to recite these mantras within your mind instead of speaking them aloud. These two tools for the mind are a powerful defense against the pull of distractions and distracting thoughts that cause disharmony to the mind's natural equanimity. When a distraction or social threat disturbs our mind's equilibrium, we can refocus and come back to the center within ourselves by reciting mentally either of these beautiful mantras. Threats come in many forms in social life, but they are obstacles only if we lose our practice of mind fasting. Reciting mantras helps us continue to fast the mind.

Another subtle obstacle to being Zen in life is when we are constantly engaged with people. This isn't to say that being in communication with people is wrong, but rather that people who thrive on meeting other people all the time, are often attracted to chitchat and gossip. Naturally those of us who seek distraction want to meet up with people all the time because the idea of fasting the mind is off-putting and almost scary. Many people are unaware that if we spend time with certain friends or colleagues *all* the time, then those relationships tend to lose vitality, which may be due in part to our adaptive psychology. When we meet up with the same people without being aware of our mind, the conversation can become stagnant and move toward idle chitchat and gossip, because we feel uncomfortable being silent in one another's presence.

On the contrary, if we spend more time by ourselves and less time socializing, we can create more space in our lives for meditation, contemplation, and creativity, which paradoxically makes our relationships more vibrant and our conversations less gossipy and more fruitful and inspired. We really have to fall in love with spending time alone and learn how to enjoy boredom in order to fast the mind. Though many of us loathe being alone or bored, both are essential for allowing the nervous system to completely reset and naturally relax. And our relationships can deepen when we realize the depth within ourselves.

Fasting the mind is the ultimate practice to cleanse our perception to live permanently in this depth. What we assume are obstacles are really only habitual patterns of being mentally attracted to distractions, regardless of whether those obstacles are perceived threats or only something to be overcome. If we embrace the methods, practices, techniques, and lifestyle of fasting the mind, then we will discover that any obstacle in our life is neither good nor bad, but instead is essential for growth. Yet we can only perceive this truth only with an equanimous mind stripped of distractive tendencies.

If something stimulates your mind to seek distraction then try another technique, but do not give up, because if you do you will miss that very important reason you are alive: to know and live from the true self, or Atman, which is the entire universe, or Brahman. To fulfill this purposeless purpose is to awaken from the depths of a mind that has completely fasted the personality away from the illusionary vapors of maya. We have finally come home to our true nature, but that nature is no place to get to. Instead it is where we've always been while we've been distracted by the mirage of our personality, thinking it was real when it didn't exist all along. Finally, our perception becomes cleansed so as to see reality as it truly *is* from a mind without deliberation.

8
FASTING THE MIND EVOKES ENLIGHTENMENT

The end result of fasting the mind is that we come back to our original, natural mind, pure consciousness, Purusha. Our samskaras have been purged and our perception cleansed as a result. We finally see the world for the first time as it truly is because we reside in our pure innate nature, which is the fundamental nature of the universe, which we call Brahman or Tao. After fasting the mind we realize that humanity erroneously perceives and thinks about the world and themselves the wrong way. This false view transforms our cognitive framework to function in accord with it. This wrong view is the linear view of the universe.

This is humanity's general view of life. We believe that things begin and end, are born and die, and so on. As a result we think that eternity, or heaven, is at the end of a period of time that we call our life. And yet how could eternity, that is, nirvana, be anywhere else but right now? It is not a product of time and so it can only be ever present. This truth was acknowledged in the East and is the core revelation of wisdom in the great spiritual traditions of Asia. It was likewise understood in the West among the Christian mystics of Europe until those mystics were killed in persecution from the twelfth through the seventeenth centuries. The truth was lost in the West as scientific inquiry began to take over spiritual matters until the point where Western religions have subtly taken on the linear view of science. This linear view is evident in the current Christian view of heaven or hell, which they consider to be at a point in time we call death. From how we educate our children to how we try to achieve our goals as adults, we view the world linearly and not naturally. Our mind is riddled with a hypnotic view of how the universe is and unfolds.

THE PROCESS OF A NATURAL MIND AND THE CONCLUSIONS OF AN UNNATURAL MIND

As humanity evolved, the West lost sight of the mind's nature, while in the East, within the great spiritual traditions, they never lost it. In the West—and in the modern world for that matter—we always seek logical conclusions to anything, as if this is how life is "figured out." We constantly collect data, losing sight of our original inquiry, as the constant upkeep of the data becomes more important. In constantly trying to figure out life we get nowhere. Our conclusions are invariably subjective, including the conclusions of science and religion, as they are according to their own dogmas. How could anybody's conclusions on any matter be accurate if they are entangled in subjectivity? This sort of problem is what Eastern thought encountered head-on. For example, what's the conclusion of a flower? What does it mean? The scientific West would be so arrogant to try to answer such an unanswerable question. The West has even applied this type of coming to conclusions for finding meaning to life itself. We often hear the question, "What is the meaning of life?" as if life has a meaning. Joseph Campbell once said:

People say that what we're all seeking is a meaning for life. I don't think that's what we're really seeking. I think that what we're seeking is an experience of being alive, so that our life experiences on the purely physical plane will have resonances with our own innermost being and reality, so that we actually feel the rapture of being alive.[1]

The Western mind has fallen headfirst into the linear view of the universe, and has applied this straight-ahead logic to all life. This linear view is a construct of our mind, bound to time, with no awareness of nature or eternity. This type of thinking comes from overcompensating for the cold cognitive controls of the mind, which detaches us from our deep-down nature. Life and the universe, then, become a linear construct that need a conclusion for us to figure it out. But as we know with a flower and a blade of grass and also life, none of these ascribe to a linear framework and instead function according to patterns and processes that are nonlinear.

Nature is fundamentally nonlinear, and our mind is a part of nature. Our mind becomes unnatural when we see the world as linear according to the conditioning of our samskaras. When we fast the mind we discover the natural, nonlinear world within our cognition because we have loosened our grip on opinions, reactions, beliefs, and the propensity to find conclusions. From the natural, nonlinear view there is only process and no conclusions. In the Eastern wisdom traditions there is a direct focus on ceasing to strive for anything, including enlightenment, because enlightenment is not a conclusion at the end of a linear process, but rather it is an enduring process that is always *now*. The Eastern sage realized it is absurd to seek and excessively strive for any conclusions if in reality the nature of everything in the universe is eternally now and thus an illusion if thought of somewhere in the distant future or past.

In China there are numerous stories that are supposed to confuse our logic so that we come back in resonance with our nature. One such story is the farmer and his son. The farmer and his son live in a small village and make their living from the farm. The father is a single parent. One day while the father was working on the farm, his only horse found a broken part of the fence and ran away. Hearing this news, the village people came to console him by saying, "How unfortunate you are." He replied, "We'll see." The next day his horse came home with two wild horses. The village people came to congratulate the farmer, saying, "How fortunate you are." He replied, "We'll see." The next day his son was riding one of the wild horses and it threw him off, causing him to break his leg. The village people again came to console the farmer, "How unfortunate you are." He again replied, "We'll see."

The next day the conscription officers came to the village, seeking men for war. When they arrived at the farmer's house they saw the son's broken leg was in a cast. So he could not go to war, nor could his father because he was the boy's only parent, while the rest of the men in the village had to leave for war. As a result all the remaining women of the village came to the farmer and expressed their joy for them, "How fortunate you are." The farmer replied, "We'll see." As the months went on the son healed but developed a terrible limp that impeded his walking. The village women came to console the farmer, "How unfortunate you are." He again replied, "We'll see." As the years went on the war came to an end but disaster had overcome the village because all the men who went to war from the village died. But like two superheroes in shining armor, the farmer and his son could continue to maintain regular labor on the farm, which was more than enough to provide for all the women of the village. In excited response the women came to express their joy to the farmer, "How fortunate we all are." Now, we all know how the farmer replied: "We'll see."

What's the point of this story? Is there a point? The purpose of this story is to make you realize that there is no definite end or conclusion to life. The story articulates that everything is process. The farmer understood that everything was process, and it is why he never got carried away or thought that his perceived good and bad fortune were ends in themselves. He is a pure man of Zen, not being blown here and there by apparent circumstances that we believe are either good or bad from our subjective viewpoint. When we recognize this as the farmer does, we discover that there is no beginning or end to the story; it just goes on ad infinitum.

The insight we realize from understanding that the universe is just natural process is that nothing is as it seems. We often emotionally get carried away with life's events as if they are ends in themselves. The story of the farmer and his son addresses such misunderstandings of life. The farmer knows nothing is as it seems and is never drawn into the temporary illusion of isolated events. He understands that there are no separate events; there is only interconnectivity. His consciousness is not stuck in the apparent duality of events that appear in the kaleidoscope of time. He has a sense of unity within himself, which is a state of perception that is cognizant of the inherent nondual nature of the universe. This is oneness in its truest form, and it is the original understanding that arose in the East. Understanding the interconnectivity of everything and the consequent nondual nature of the universe is the gift that the East gave the world—and continues to do so through their spiritual traditions.

The way to come back in accord with this eternal reality requires a certain level of confusion for our common linear and logical state of mind that we continue to promote. As with the farmer and his son, the story is designed to puzzle your mind out of any conclusions as to what the story means. Instead it evokes your natural mind, which is only process without finality. This art of puzzling the mind out of its usual linearity is a primary tool for fasting the mind back into its original enlightened nature.

THE MYSTICS' IRRATIONAL VIEW OF THE UNIVERSE

In the East the irrational view is commended with high praise, and rational logic and conclusions are secondary to that. The mystics and sages of the East realized that if someone is to experience the splendor and beauty of the ultimate reality (Brahman or Tao) in life as they do, then their rational attempts to do so must be extinguished. To achieve a state of equanimity, we must weed out logic from our mind so that the search for conclusions withers away.

This problem is not only part of the Western world and the modern era; it also existed in the ancient East, and it is why the mystics and sages came up with clever methods to puzzle the mind, just like the old Chinese tale of the farmer and his son. These methods, in some sense, are extremely sophisticated and appear well thought out. But it is most likely they are spontaneous utterances of a pure mind answering a rational question with an irrational answer. We discover such irrationality in a famous story of a monk who asked his master, Tung-shan Shou-ch'u, "What is the Buddha?" Tung-shan Shou-ch'u replied, "Three pounds of flax."

Some scholars suggest that Tung-shan Shou-ch'u was weighing flax at this moment and gave a spontaneous response. Though this is somewhat plausible, it is not truly the parable behind his response. The reason for Tung-shan Shou-ch'u's irrational answer is exactly that: it cannot be understood logically and as a result, like being hit with a whip, we come back to our natural awareness and attention, which is beyond the world of thinking. Tung-shan Shou-ch'u essentially answered the monk's question in a roundabout way because that state of consciousness beyond the linear world of thought and rationality in this very moment is the Buddha's state of consciousness.

This technique is popular in the Zen Buddhist tradition of East Asia, especially in China, Korea, and Japan. Such encounters are known as *koans* in Japanese. The koan is a story, dialogue, statement, and ultimately a riddle, which is used in Zen practice to provoke great doubt in the student's mind to test their progress in Zen. One of the oldest koans can be found in the *Chuang-tzu* text, and this is why some scholars believe Zen Buddhism is a tradition built in part on the wisdom of the great Taoist sage Chuang-tzu. In this passage Chuang-tzu uses complete nonsense to puzzle our intellectual faculties so that we stand back in awe and are brought back to the ground of the irrational impartiality of life:

> There is a beginning. There is a not yet beginning to be a beginning. There is a not yet beginning to be a not yet beginning to be a beginning. There is being. There is nonbeing. There is a not yet beginning to be nonbeing. There is a not yet beginning to be a not yet beginning to be nonbeing. Suddenly there is nonbeing.[2]

Wow! Trying to make sense of such a passage is impossible—and that's precisely the point. Actually, Chuang-tzu is using pure humor as well in this passage, because even in his day people tried to use logic to understand the meaning of the universe and our very existence, only to arrive at erroneous conclusions.

Koans are famously employed by Zen masters to throw disciples back into the present moment, where process has no beginning or end, because thinking has completely succumbed to the irrational view, as we discover in the *Chuang-tzu* passage.

One such encounter with a koan is a story where a disciple was summoned to the Zen master's home. The Zen master, in true koan fashion, told the disciple that he wanted an exhibition of Zen tomorrow. Leaving the master's quarters the disciple was confused as to how such an exhibition of Zen could be showcased. That whole night the disciple tossed and turned in bed, anxious about how to please the master. The next day, on the way to the master's home, the disciple was still fretting about how to exhibit Zen when he saw a unique frog that is a native of Japan. "Aha!" he thought. Taking the frog to the master he was sure this would be sufficient enough. When he arrived at the master's home the master asked, "So can you exhibit Zen to me?" In reply, the disciple showed the master the frog. The master gave a slight smirk and said, "No, too intellectual." In other words, his exhibition was too contrived, too thought out. The very thinking about it thwarted the project. To answer the master somewhat authentically in this regard requires no thinking, as Zen is the natural spontaneity of the universe in the eternal now. So to exhibit Zen is not to worry about it, because Zen is life.

To exhibit Zen and gain the master's approval would be to achieve the purpose of the koan, which is to fall into the irrational sphere of spontaneity in the present moment. For example, another Zen koan describes a master who placed a pitcher before two disciples. The master said, "Do not call it a pitcher, but tell me what it is." One disciple replied, "It cannot be called a piece of wood." The master was not at all satisfied with this response. He turned to the other disciple, who simply knocked the pitcher over and walked away as if nothing happened. The master was extremely pleased with the second disciple's actions. The second disciple gained full approval for his understanding of life, which is Zen. Some may say that this approach of the riddle in the East, especially in Zen teaching, is utter buffoonery and nonsense, and the teachers themselves are mere buffoons. But this is only the way it appears to a highly rational mind seeking meaning in a world that is truly beyond meaning. Bound by mental complexity, many of us believe life equates to our conditioned thoughts about it. Nothing could be further from the truth, and this is why the so-called buffoonery is true genius at exposing the actual buffoon in this world: your personality built by linear time.

The wisdom of the East reveals that the reality of life is really simple, and its nature is your own nature, which is originally enlightened. This is Zen in its purest form. Realizing this natural simplicity in life is expressed in the koan of Zen master Chao-chou Ts'ung-shen and a new disciple who just arrived at his monastery. The disciple asked, "I have just entered the monastery. Please give me instructions." Ts'ung-shen said, "Have you had your breakfast?" "Yes, I have," replied the disciple. "Then," said Ts'ung-shen, "wash your bowls."

In hearing these words the disciple gained insight, and it is commonly thought that the disciple was instantly enlightened. There was nothing to grasp, nothing to seek; it was always there in the ordinary life that we too often seek to escape. Yet the place we should be trying to escape, or transcend, is the habit of the linear mind, which keeps us blind to the majesty of our eternally present enlightened nature. When we come home, so to speak, to that ever-present place within our consciousness, then we have become one with the ultimate reality—but this is not really true because it implies the dualistic idea that you and Brahman or Tao were separate. In truth, you have just awakened to the fact that Brahman was always your identity, as is everyone else's. This recognition releases our being from the illusionary prison of the mind to its innate freedom. This liberation from the rational into the irrational is expressed as naturalness, which in Chinese is called *tzu-jan* (自然), through the individual. It is the intelligent spontaneity, *wu-wei,* which is evoked from a mind of no deliberation. This is the intelligence of the universe expressed through the mind, called *buddhi* in Sanskrit.

In ancient Japanese fencing naturalness is recognized in the same manner as Zen is recognized through the koan. When an aspiring fencer arrives at the master's home to learn fencing, the master tells them to forget about using the fencing weapons or learning any techniques and instead concentrate on washing the dishes. Every day the fencing disciple washes the dishes. As the disciple cleans the dishes the master comes out of nowhere and hits them in the head. The next day the disciple is preparing their defense for a head shot, and then the master comes from a different direction to surprise the disciple with a swift hit to the ribs. This goes on for weeks, as the disciple continually plans their defense. After many weeks, the disciple realizes that all their efforts to conjure a defense are futile, and as a result, they learn to let go. In letting go the disciple ceases thinking and comes to a place of equanimity in the mind. This state of consciousness is a poise of absolute centeredness and natural spontaneous response. Once the disciple is in this natural state, the master can come from any direction, and the disciple can defend themself without having to plan it. This is the art of fencing, but also the art of life.

A great example of this state of consciousness is Forrest Gump. In the *Forrest Gump* film, Gump (played by Tom Hanks) was ironically a simpleminded man who went on to achieve many great accomplishments in his life without having to think about them or plan ahead. He became a football player, war hero, Ping-Pong champion, shrimping boat captain and founder of the Bubba Gump Shrimp Company, and he loved Jenny unquestionably even when she appeared disinterested in him. Through all of his trials and tribulations, Forrest Gump approached life with the naturalness of a Zen master or fencing champion. He truly lived by his mother's motto: "Mama said life was like a box of chocolates. You never know what you're gonna get." Gump never felt the urge to resist change, and so he flowed through life like a feather, like the Taoist sage Lao-tzu. Many of us resist change and suffer as a result, which keeps us locked away from the divine ultimate reality that Forrest Gump lived in. In not resisting change he lived his mama's motto to the fullest. He became the perfect man, according to the wisdom of Chuang-tzu. His mind was a replica of Chuang-tzu's mirror mind, which is the state of mind that appears after fasting the mind:

Do not be an embodier of fame; do not be a storehouse of schemes; do not undertake of projects; do not be a proprietor of wisdom. Embody to the fullest what has no end and wander where there is no trail. Hold on to all that you have received from Heaven but do not think you have gotten anything. Be empty, that is all. The Perfect Man uses his mind like a mirror—going after nothing, welcoming nothing, responding but not storing. Therefore he can win out over things and not hurt himself.[3]

Having this post-fasting naturalness of the mirror mind, essentially the effortless mind of Forrest Gump, doesn't mean we don't feel or have emotions. On the contrary, we feel more and our emotions are sensitive, but we are not emotional, that is, we do not react egotistically to life's circumstances. The naturalness evoked by the mirror mind, essentially

Figure 8.1. Bhumisparsha mudra. Photo taken by Jason Gregory at Wat Si Saket (Si Saket Temple) in Vientiane, Laos.

the fasted mind, is the immovable place of the Buddha. This immovable place is the natural state of consciousness that we return to when we practice mind fasting sincerely to its fullest potential.

The immovable place is the naturalness of the Japanese fencer, Zen master, and the great sages of ancient times. The winds of drama in the world will try to infect your soul by gravitationally pulling your attention out of your center and into the outside world, where samskaras are born and the wheel of samsara continues to make you suffer day after day, year after year, and life after life. But when you reside in the immovable place, the tornado of worldly delusion cannot move you, and as a result you finally realize the wisdom behind the mind fasting practice of neti neti, "not this, not that." In fasting the mind back to this original state you become the pure witness, Purusha, untouched by the seduction and temptation of the dual world, prakrti. The eternal witness of this immovable place is symbolized in Buddhism with the hand gesture of the *Bhumisparsha mudra* (see figure 8.1) in which the Buddha touches the earth with his hand, calling upon the earth itself to witness his enlightenment.

But fasting the mind and its eventual realization of the immovable place is not to become a stone Buddha. It is an unstuck psychological state that is best explained with the Japanese word *unsui* (雲水), which refers to cloud and water. For the enlightened mind drifts like a cloud and flows like water.

NOTES

INTRODUCTION. THE CURE IS ANCIENT

1. Watts, *The Book*, 39.
2. *Bhagavad Gita*, 136.

1. THE NEED FOR SPEED IS SUICIDE

1. Hanh, *Silence*, 25, 47, 48.
2. Feinberg, "Christopher Nolan."

2. WAR ON THE NERVOUS SYSTEM

1. Hart, *The Art of Living*, 74, 75.
2. Campbell, *Pathways to Bliss*, 119.
3. Hart, *The Art of Living*, 91, 92.
4. Hanh, *Silence*, 25, 26, 27.
5. Confucius, *Analects*, 178, 179.
6. Ibid., 179.

3. CULTURAL AND HISTORICAL BACKGROUND

1. Huxley, *The Perennial Philosophy*, 271.

2. Upanishads, 68.

3. Maharshi, *Be as You Are,* 131.

4. Watts, *The Way of Zen,* 26.

5. Chuang Tzu, *Complete Works,* 5–6.

6. Ibid., 57, 58.

7. Slingerland, *Trying Not to Try,* 161, 162.

4. THE ANCIENT SCIENCE OF MIND FASTING

1. Maharshi, *Be as You Are,* 195, 32.

2. Ibid., 180.

3. Campbell, *The Power of Myth,* 29.

4. Campbell, *Myths of Light,* 46.

5. Hart, *Art of Living,* 107, 108.

6. Patanjali, *Yoga-Sutra,* 9.

7. Ibid., 6, 7.

8. Lao-tzu, *Tao Te Ching.*

5. THE MODERN SCIENCE OF MIND FASTING

1. Slingerland, *Trying Not to Try,* 28.

2. Nisbett, *The Geography of Thought,* 34, 35.

3. Ibid., 38.

4. Slingerland, *Trying Not to Try,* 63, 64.

5. Mencius, https://simple.wikipedia.org/wiki/Ox_Mountain.

6. DOWNREGULATING THE SENSE OF "I" WITH MIND FASTING

1. Dyer, *Wisdom of the Ages,* 35.

2. Slingerland, *Trying Not to Try,* 102.

3. Ibid., 187, 188.

4. Chuang-tzu, *Complete Works,* 50, 51.

5. Slingerland, *Trying Not to Try,* 29.

7. THE ART OF PRACTICING
MIND FASTING

1. Capra, *Tao of Physics,* 124.

2. Perlmutter, "Preventing Alzheimer's."

3. Perlmutter, "How Can Eating Gluten Affect the Health of My Brain?"

4. Gulati and Misra, "Sugar Intake, Obesity, and Diabetes in India"; "Sugarcane," en.wikipedia.org/wiki/Sugarcane#Production; "World Map," www.mapsofworld.com/world-top-ten/world-map-countries-wheat-production.html; Carroll, "Top 10 Largest Wheat Producing Countries"; and Mascarenhas, "World Health Day."

5. Kelly, *The Yin and Yang of Climate Crisis,* 54, 55.

6. Newport, *Deep Work,* 3.

7. Ibid., 12.

8. Tenzin Gyatso (Fourteenth Dalai Lama), "On the Meaning of: OM MANI PADME HUM."

8. FASTING THE MIND EVOKES
ENLIGHTENMENT

1. Campbell, *Power of Myth,* 4, 5.

2. Chuang-tzu, *Complete Works,* 43.

3. Ibid., 97.

BIBLIOGRAPHY

Austin, James. *Zen and the Brain: Toward an Understanding of Meditation and Consciousness*. Cambridge, Mass.: MIT Press, 1999.

Beilock, Sian. *Choke: What the Secrets of the Brain Reveal about Getting It Right When You Have To*. New York: Free Press, 2010.

Benoit, Hubert. *Zen and the Psychology of Transformation: The Supreme Doctrine*. Rochester, Vt.: Inner Traditions, 1990.

Blofeld, John. *Taoism: Road to Immortality*. Boston: Shambhala Publications, 2000.

Campbell, Joseph. *Myths of Light: Eastern Metaphors of the Eternal*. Novato, Calif.: New World Library, 2003.

———. *Pathways to Bliss: Mythology and Personal Transformation*. Novato, Calif.: New World Library, 2004.

———. *The Power of Myth*. New York: Anchor Books, 1991.

Capra, Fritjof. *The Tao of Physics: An Exploration of the Parallels Between Modern Physics and Eastern Mysticism*. Boston: Shambhala Publications, 2000.

Carroll, Nancy. "Top 10 Largest Wheat Producing Countries in the World." CountryDetail, www.countrydetail.com/top-10-largest-wheat-producing -countries-world/.

Chuang-tzu. *The Complete Works of Chuang Tzu*. Translated by Burton Watson. New York: Columbia University Press, 1968.

Clark, Andy. *Being There: Putting Brain, Body, and World Together Again.* Cambridge, Mass.: MIT Press, 1997.

Cleary, Thomas. *The Taoism Reader.* Boston: Shambhala Publications, 2012.

Confucius. *Analects: With Selections from Traditional Commentaries.* Translated by Edward Slingerland. Indianapolis: Hackett Publishing, 2003.

Csikszentmihalyi, Mihaly. *Flow: The Psychology of Optimal Experience.* New York: Harper and Row, 1990.

Dennett, Daniel. *Consciousness Explained.* Boston: Back Bay Books, 1991.

Dietrich, Arne. *Introduction to Consciousness.* London: Palgrave Macmillan, 2007.

Durkheim, Emile. *The Elementary Forms of Religious Life.* New York: Oxford, 2008.

Dyer, Wayne W. *Wisdom of the Ages: 60 Days to Enlightenment.* New York: William Morrow, 2002.

Easwaran, Eknath, trans. *The Upanishads: A Classic of Indian Spirituality.* Tomales, Calif.: Nilgiri Press, 2007.

Feinberg, Scott. "Christopher Nolan on 'Interstellar' Critics, Making Original Films and Shunning Cellphones and Email (Q&A)." *The Hollywood Reporter,* January 3, 2015, www.hollywoodreporter.com/race /christopher-nolan-interstellar-critics-making-760897.

Flanagan, Owen. *The Bodhisattva's Brain: Buddhism Naturalized.* New York: Bradford Books, 2011.

Gregory, Jason. *Enlightenment Now: Liberation Is Your True Nature.* Rochester, Vt.: Inner Traditions, 2016.

———. *The Science and Practice of Humility: The Path to Ultimate Freedom.* Rochester, Vt.: Inner Traditions, 2014.

Griffith, Ralph T. H. *The Hymns of the Rgveda: Translated in English with a Popular Commentary.* Delhi: Motilal Banarsidass Publishers, 1999.

Gulati, Seema, and Anoop Misra, "Sugar Intake, Obesity, and Diabetes in India." *Nutrients* 6, no. 12 (Dec 2014): 5955–5947, www.ncbi.nlm.nih.gov /pmc/articles/PMC4277009/#B21-nutrients-06-05955.

Guenon, Rene. *The Essential Rene Guenon: Metaphysics, Tradition, and the Crisis of Modernity.* Bloomington, Ind.: World Wisdom, Inc., 2009.

Gyatso, Tenzin (Fourteenth Dalai Lama). "On the Meaning of: OM MANI

PADME HUM." Transcribed by Ngawang Tashi (Taswa), Drepung Loseling, Mungod, India, www.sacred-texts.com/bud/tib/omph.htm.

Hanh, Thich Nhat. *Silence: The Power of Quiet in a World Full of Noise.* London: Rider, 2015.

Hanson, Rick. *Buddha's Brain: The Practical Neuroscience of Happiness, Love, and Wisdom.* Oakland, Calif.: New Harbinger Publications Inc., 2009.

Hart, William. *The Art of Living: Vipassana Meditation.* New York: Harper One, 1987.

Holman, John. *The Return of the Perennial Philosophy: The Supreme Vision of Western Esotericism.* London: Watkins, 2008.

Huxley, Aldous. *The Perennial Philosophy.* New York: Harper Perennial Modern Classics, 2009.

Ivanhoe, Philip J. and Bryan W. Van Norden, *Readings in Classical Chinese Philosophy.* Indianapolis: Hackett Publishing Company, 2005.

Ivanhoe, Philip J. *The Daodejing of Laozi.* Indianapolis: Hackett Publishing Company, 2003.

Kelly, Brendan. *The Yin and Yang of Climate Crisis: Healing Personal, Cultural, and Ecological Imbalance with Chinese Medicine.* Berkeley, Calif.: North Atlantic Books, 2015.

Kingsley, Peter. *Reality.* Point Reyes, Calif.: The Golden Sufi Center, 2004.

Krishnamurti, Jiddu. *Krishnamurti: Reflections on the Self.* Chicago: Open Court, 1998.

———. *Total Freedom: The Essential Krishnamurti.* New York: Harper One, 1996.

Lao-tzu. *Tao Te Ching: An Illustrated Journey.* Translated by Stephen Mitchell. London: Frances Lincoln, 2009.

Maharshi, Sri Ramana. *Be as You Are: The Teaching of Sri Ramana Maharshi.* Translated by David Godman. Delhi: Penguin Books, 1992.

———. *Saddarsanam and An Inquiry into the Revelation of Truth and Oneself.* Translated by Nome. Santa Cruz, Calif: Society of Abidance in Truth, 2009.

Mascarenhas, Anuradha. "World Health Day: India among Top 3 Countries with High Diabetic Population." The Indian Express, indianexpress .com/article/lifestyle/health/diabetes-cases-422-mn-worldwide-india-no -2-who-lancet-world-health-day/.

Masters, Robert Augustus. *Spiritual Bypassing: When Spirituality Disconnects*

Us from What Really Matters. Berkeley, Calif.: North Atlantic Books, 2010.

Mengzi. *Mengzi.* Translated by Bryan W. Van Norden. Indianapolis: Hackett Publishing, 2008.

Merton, Thomas. *The Way of Chuang Tzu.* New York: New Directions, 2010.

Newport, Cal. *Deep Work: Rules for Focused Success in a Distracted World.* New York: Grand Central Publishing, 2016.

Nisbett, Richard E. *The Geography of Thought: How Asians and Westerners Think Differently . . . and Why.* New York: Free Press, 2003.

Ouspensky, P. D. *In Search of the Miraculous: The Teachings of G. I. Gurdjieff.* Orlando, Fla.: Harcourt, 2001.

Patanjali. *The Yoga-Sutra of Patanjali.* Translated with commentary by Chip Hartranft. Boston: Shambhala Publications, 2003.

Perlmutter, David. "How Can Eating Gluten Affect the Health of My Brain?" davidperlmutter MD, www.drperlmutter.com/can-eating-gluten-affect -health-brain/.

———. "Preventing Alzheimer's and Other Brain Illnesses." davidperlmutter MD, www.drperlmutter.com/preventing-alzheimers-brain-illnesses/.

Pine, Red. *The Heart Sutra.* Berkeley, Calif.: Counterpoint, 2005.

———. *The Zen Teachings of Bodhidharma.* Berkeley, Calif.: North Point Press, 1989.

Pinker, Steven. *How the Mind Works.* New York: W. W. Norton and Company Inc., 1997.

———. *The Language Instinct: How the Mind Creates Language.* New York: Harper Perennial Modern Classics, 2007.

Radhakrishnan, Sarvepalli. *The Bhagavadgita.* Noida, India: HarperCollins India, 2010.

Ramacharaka, Yogi. *Advance Course in Yogi Philosophy and Oriental Occultism.* Chicago: The Yogi Publication Society, 1931.

———. *Fourteen Lessons in Yogi Philosophy and Oriental Occultism.* Chicago: The Yogi Publication Society, 1931.

———. *Lessons in Gnani Yoga: The Yoga of Wisdom.* Chicago: The Yogi Publication Society, 1934.

Schuon, Frithjof. *The Transcendent Unity of Religions.* Wheaton, Ill.: Quest Books, 1984.

Shankara. *Shankara's Crest Jewel of Discrimination*. Translated by Swami Prabhavananda and Christopher Isherwood. Los Angeles: Vedanta Society of Southern California, 1975.

Slingerland, Edward and Mark Collard, editors. *Creating Consilience: Integrating the Sciences and the Humanities*. New York: Oxford, 2012.

Slingerland, Edward. *Trying Not to Try: Ancient China, Modern Science, and the Power of Spontaneity*. New York: Broadway Books, 2014.

"Sugarcane." Wikipedia, en.wikipedia.org/wiki/Sugarcane#Production.

Suzuki, Daisetz Teitaro, trans. *The Lankavatara Sutra: A Mahayana Text*. Philadelphia, Pa.: Coronet Books, 1999.

Suzuki, Shunryu. *Zen Mind, Beginner's Mind*. Boston: Shambhala Publications, 2011.

Tsu, Chuang. *Chuang Tsu: Inner Chapters, A Companion Volume to Tao Te Ching*. Translated by Gia-Fu Feng and Jane English. Portland, Ore.: Amber Lotus, 2008.

Upanishads. Translated by Patrick Olivelle. New York: Oxford, 1996.

Watts, Alan. *Become What You Are*. Boston: Shambhala Publications, 2003.

———. *The Book: On the Taboo Against Knowing Who You Are*. New York: Vintage Books, 1989.

———. *Do You Do It, or Does It Do You: How to Let the Universe Meditate You*. Audio CD. Louisville, Colo.: Sounds True, 2005.

———. *Out of Your Mind: Essential Listening from the Alan Watts Audio Archives*. Audio CD. Louisville, Colo.: Sounds True, 2004.

———. *Tao: The Watercourse Way*. New York: Pantheon, 1977.

———. *The Way of Zen*. New York: Vintage Books, 1999.

———. *The Wisdom of Insecurity: A Message for an Age of Anxiety*. New York: Vintage Books, 2011.

Welwood, John. *Perfect Love, Imperfect Relationships: Healing the Wound of the Heart*. Boston: Trumpeter Books, 2007.

———. *Toward a Psychology of Awakening: Buddhism, Psychotherapy, and the Path of Personal and Spiritual Transformation*. Boston: Shambhala Publications, 2002.

Wilhelm, Richard. *The I Ching or Book of Changes*. Princeton, N.J.: Princeton University Press, 1967.

———. *The Secret of the Golden Flower: A Chinese Book of Life*. London: Arkana, 1984.

"World Map with Top Ten Countries by Wheat Production." Maps of World, www.mapsofworld.com/world-top-ten/world-map-countries-wheat -production.html.

Xunzi. *Xunzi*. Translated by Burton Watson. New York: Columbia University Press, 2003.

Yee, Colleen Saidman. *Yoga for Life: A Journey to Inner Peace and Freedom*. New York: Atria, 2015.

Yukteswar, Swami Sri. *The Holy Science*. Los Angeles: Self-Realization Fellowship, 1990.

INDEX